DINING IN-
MONTEREY PENINSULA

A Collection of Gourmet Recipes from Monterey
Peninsula's Finest Restaurants

By Regina Hicks, John Hicks and Corneles Van Peski

With a Foreword by Merv Griffin

PEANUT BUTTER PUBLISHING

Peanut Butter Towers   Seattle, Washington 98134

Cover Photography by Dale Windham

CONTENTS

FOREWORD

The fame of the Monterey Peninsula is deserved; a 'must' on the travel plans of Americans and, for that matter, tourists from every corner of the world. This breathtaking pocket of the California coast contains the 'best features' of the glamour resorts of the world. No matter where I travel in the world, when I reveal the location of my home, it never fails to evoke a gasp and "that's my favorite place in America." It leaves a lasting picture in the mind of the traveler.

It's the kind of beauty spot that has enticed the artists and craftsmen of the world . . . and with the migration of the gifted ones comes the migration of some of the world's most honored talents . . . the chefs. For a community with a population of 247,450, the yellow pages of the telephone book contain 29 pages dedicated to the restaurants of the Monterey Peninsula.

Unique also in this setting is the fact that many of the great agricultural areas of California are less than a half-hour's drive away. The lettuce fields of Salinas . . . the 'artichoke capital of the world,' Castroville . . . the vineyards of Monterey giving us great wines of California . . . and add to it the blue waters of the Monterey Bay and the Pacific Ocean and you have a gastronomer's paradise: fresh salmon, abalone, Monterey prawns, Garrapata trout, rock cod, swordfish! And the wild boar is another taste treat of the Peninsula.

The restaurants and their chefs featured in this book are deservedly the 'heavyweights' of our community . . . but let me also share with you some delicious 'stops' that only we residents know of . . .

A breakfast at the Wagon Wheel in the little shopping center not far up the Carmel Valley Road would be the heartiest meal in the tradition of a pioneer's breakfast. And don't be surprised to see Doris Day at the counter and Clint Eastwood wandering in.

How about fresh fish and white wine for lunch on Fisherman's Wharf in Monterey at Abalonetti's, recommended even by National Geographic magazine? I've sat next to Liv Ullman and Gene Hackman at that little spot . . . out of the Bay and into your mouth in less than an hour.

How about a leisurely drive south on Route 1 to Big Sur and a fabulous luncheon at Ventana . . . sitting on the side of the Big Sur Mountain looking a hundred miles down the rugged coastline on a warm afternoon . . . or right down the road from Ventana to Nepenthe, sitting in the house that Orson Welles built for Rita Hayworth and where Henry Miller spent many days during his residence in Big Sur?

And where do all the restaurant owners want to be invited to sup? I'll tell you where . . . to John Gardiner's Tennis Ranch in Carmel Valley. The luncheons and dinners are world famous with heads of state, leaders of industry, movie stars, Arthur and Kathryn Murray and Herb Caen. Don't plan on going, though . . . it's private—members and those clients working out in the tennis clinics only. You can't imagine what it's like to serve a ball after you've been served Gardiner's famous Strawberry Soufflé.

The Thunderbird Bookstore at the mouth of the Carmel Valley is another local favorite—unique in the fact that your eyes can browse among the books while your stomach enjoys a tasty luncheon.

If you're not in the mood for the confines of a restaurant and its service, how about a do-it-yourself meal? Go to the Mediterranean Market on Ocean Avenue in Carmel and have them prepare you the world's greatest picnic lunch with delicacies from everywhere in the world. Go sit on the fabulous white sands of Carmel Beach and think about the dinner you're going to have that night.

Did I tell you about the Tuck Box in Carmel? Just try and get in that door any morning! Their popovers and jam have always been the talk of the town . . . and don't be surprised to see Hansel and Gretel walk in the door; it looks exactly like their house . . . which leads me to the decorations and settings of all of these dining spots. No two are alike; some are very European in decor and some very Californian. But most of all, the customer counts! The warmth and the desire to please that customer is evident everywhere.

Look cool when you accidentally bump into one of our famous residents. I've already mentioned a few, but Paul Anka and his adorable family are often 'out on the town' . . . General Jimmy Doolittle is now a member of the community . . . Jean Arthur magically appears . . . as does the tennis star Helen Wills Moody . . . and Doug McClure is in and out of everywhere. And, if a very distinguished man is sitting across the room, it could be the master photographer Ansel Adams, or it could be the renowned sculptor, Malcolm Moran. You'll be traveling the same streets where Robert Louis Stevenson, John Steinbeck and Robinson Jeffers often strolled.

It's a community of style, creativity and great beauty. Enjoy these pages devoted to our admired citizens . . . the chefs.

Your friend in good food,

Merv Griffin

ABOUT THE AUTHORS

Since 1964, when Regina and John Hicks moved from Dallas to Carmel, they have concentrated their talents on writing and photography. Their published works include *Monterey: A Pictorial History* and *Cannery Row: A Pictorial History,* both of which are highly successful historical photo-essay publications.

Their avocation, however, has been a dedication to researching culinary delights throughout the United States, Canada and Mexico. In spite of a continual need to fight 'the battle of the bulge,' John and Regina have found more wonderful and varied restaurants on the Monterey Peninsula, within a more compact area, than anyplace else in their travels. They are convinced that the quality of 'chef-dom' found in the Peninsula is unsurpassed anywhere.

'Van,' as Corneles Van Peski is known to his friends, was born and grew up in Holland. After graduating from high school he apprenticed in the grand manner at the Hotel Hamdorff in Laren, where he specialized in the techniques of making fine pastries, breads and cakes. He continued his education at the Grand Hotel Den Doelen in The Hague, learning European and French cuisine. He spent another year at the Indonesian Hotel Restaurant picking up the finer points of Indonesian cooking before coming to the United States in 1931.

Van's experience in this country has been extensive, including nine years at The Lodge in Pebble Beach, two years at the Hob-Nob in Carmel, then to the Outrigger, and finally eighteen years as executive chef at Neil de Vaughn's before retiring in 1976. Since his retirement Van has been working harder than ever—making the finest croissants in the world, teaching, writing, helping new lovers of the art of cooking get a start and, for a slight charge, cooking for private parties.

Bertolucci

Dinner for Four

Oysters Belvedere with Scarpara Sauce

Minestrone Soup

Romaine or Butter Lettuce Salad
with
Bertolucci's Dressing

Vitello Ducale

Eggplant Dorate

Spumoni

Wines:

With Appetizer: Soave Classico
With Entrée: Berlucchi Pinot di Fraciacorta or Barberani Orvieto
With Dessert or After-Dinner: Bonardi Asti Spumante

Dino and Claudia Bertolucci, Owners
Claudia Bertolucci, Maître d'
Dino Bertolucci, Chef

Bertolucci is located on Forest Avenue, just off Lighthouse Avenue in downtown Pacific Grove, but a glance at the menu will transport you to Northern Italy.

Chef Dino Bertolucci, whose love for cooking was instilled early by his teacher in Genoa, chef Gofredo Fraccaro, speaks with contagious enthusiasm about food and food preparation. With his wife Claudia he opened this intimate sixty-seat restaurant in 1974, and has been catering to eighty percent repeat customers ever since. With a warm welcome from Claudia and daughter Eleanor to the two tastefully appointed dining rooms displaying lovely tables set with fine quality white linens and gleaming silver, the stage is set for Dino's excellent Northern Italian cuisine.

Everything about this friendly, unpretentious restaurant reflects the Bertolucci family's philosophy. As Claudia puts it, "We care about people, not about the cash register."

208 Forest Avenue
Pacific Grove

OYSTERS BELVEDERE

24 small to medium-sized oysters
1 cup flour
1 egg, beaten
1 teaspoon finely chopped parsley
1 tablespoon lemon juice
Breadcrumbs, finely ground
1 tablespoon grated Parmesan cheese
1/2 teaspoon finely chopped fresh sweet basil
Scarpara Sauce
4 thin slices French bread, halved, buttered and toasted

1. Bread oysters by dipping first into flour, then into beaten egg mixed
   with chopped parsley and lemon juice, then into finely ground breadcrumbs mixed with Parmesan cheese and basil.
2. Grill on lightly oiled grill or in a sauté pan until just golden in color.
   Remove.
3. Place grilled oysters into *Scarpara Sauce* and simmer from 5 to 7
   minutes. Remove to serving plate.
4. Serve immediately with toasted halves of French bread.

SCARPARA SAUCE

***Prepare this sauce a day ahead to allow time for the flavors
to blend properly.***

3 to 4 pounds fresh tomatoes, ground or blended smooth
1 teaspoon finely chopped fresh sweet basil
1 teaspoon lemon juice
1 ounce white wine
1 ounce dry sherry
1 cup cold water, if needed for proper consistency
2 teaspoons finely chopped parsley

1. Combine all ingredients except water and parsley. Bring to a boil,
   then lower heat to simmer and continue cooking 12 to 14 hours,
   stirring occasionally. *Add water only if necessary.*
2. Add parsley during the last half-hour of cooking.

***Adding the parsley too early will destroy the texture of the
seasoning and will darken the sauce.***

MINESTRONE SOUP

2-1/2 to 3 gallons cold water
1 cup white navy beans
1 zucchini, diced
2 stalks celery, diced
1 white onion, chopped
1 bunch spinach, chopped
2 fresh tomatoes, chopped
1 potato, diced
2 teaspoons finely chopped fresh sweet basil
Salt and pepper to taste
4 teaspoons olive oil

Combine all ingredients, bring to a boil and then lower heat to simmer.
Continue cooking for 12 hours.

***The secret to fine minestrone is dicing vegetables very small,
beginning with cold water, and simmering very slowly for the full time.
The volume will diminish to serve four.***

ROMAINE OR BUTTER LETTUCE SALAD

1. Select lettuce leaf by leaf. Use only perfect leaves. Wash thoroughly and dry in colander. Cover with damp cloth and set in refrigerator to crisp.
2. When ready to serve, tear greens into bite-size pieces and toss lightly with *Dressing*.

BERTOLUCCI SALAD DRESSING

3/4 cup salad oil
3 ounces vinegar
2 teaspoons olive oil
2 teaspoons lemon juice
1/2 teaspoon prepared mustard
1 teaspoon finely chopped parsley
3/4 teaspoon salt
1/2 teaspoon pepper, or to taste
1/4 teaspoon dry oregano
1/4 teaspoon dry sweet basil
1 teaspoon finely chopped or grated white onion

Blend all ingredients with wire whisk. Store in refrigerator at least 24 hours before using.

VITELLO DUCALE

Prepare *Fish Stock* and *Fish Sauce* in advance.

8 scallops or slices of veal, 3 to 4-ounces each
Salt and pepper to taste
Pinch finely chopped parsley
Pinch finely chopped oregano
4 jumbo prawns, shelled, cleaned and butterflied—with shells reserved
1 cup flour
1 egg, beaten
Fish Sauce
8 mushroom caps
1 ounce brandy or sherry
Garnish: 4 sprigs fresh parsley

1. Preheat oven to 375 degrees.
2. Lightly pound veal scallops and sprinkle each with salt, pepper, parsley and oregano.
3. Dip prepared prawns into flour, then into beaten egg and grill quickly on lightly oiled grill or in sauté pan until just golden. Remove.
4. Place 1 grilled prawn on top of each of 4 slices of veal. Cover with remaining slices of veal and steady each serving with tooth picks on all 4 sides.
5. Dip each serving into flour, coating both sides, then quickly in and out of egg batter. Grill on both sides until golden. Remove and hold.
6. Line bottom of individual casseroles or 1 large baking dish with half of the *Fish Sauce*. Layer veal servings on top of sauce. Garnish with mushroom caps and top with remaining sauce.
7. Just before placing in oven, pour brandy or sherry over top. Bake in preheated oven for 15 to 20 minutes.
8. Garnish with sprigs of parsley and serve.

FISH SAUCE

3/4 cup butter
3/4 cup flour
Salt and pepper to taste
Fish Stock

1. Melt butter and mix in flour to make roux. Add salt and pepper to taste. Blend over low heat for at least 5 minutes, but do not brown.
2. Slowly pour in hot *Fish Stock*, stirring to blend and then cooking rapidly for 5 minutes until creamy. Strain through a sieve to assure that sauce is smooth.

DINO'S FISH STOCK

1 pound filet of sole, or other white fish
Prawn shells
1 onion, cut into quarters
2 stalks celery
1 lemon, cut in half
3 bay leaves
4 ounces white wine
4 ounces cooking sherry
1 to 1-1/2 gallons cold water

Bring all ingredients to a boil. Reduce heat and simmer for at least 4 hours, reducing stock to approximately 7 cups.

Always begin with cold water.

A fine chef always uses his imagination to create new dishes. *Vitello Ducale* is my own creation.

EGGPLANT DORATE

1 eggplant, peeled
1/2 cup flour
2 eggs, beaten
Salt and pepper to taste
Sweet basil, oregano and finely chopped parsley

1. Cut 4 slices 3/4" thick from center of eggplant. Dip in flour, then
   in beaten egg to cover.
2. Grill on lightly oiled griddle or saute' pan for 3 to 4 minutes
   on both sides. Do not overcook.
3. Salt and pepper to taste and top with a pinch of sweet basil,
   oregano and finely chopped parsley.

Spumoni should be prepared at least 24 hours in advance.

SPUMONI

1 cup each of three different flavors of ice cream
1-1/2 cups of a fourth flavor of ice cream
2 ounces whipping cream
3/4 teaspoon sugar
3/4 teaspoon Marsala wine
3/4 teaspoon brandy
1/2 cup glacé fruit, finely chopped
Saran wrap

1. Using a 1-quart mold, cover bottom with one flavor of ice cream.
2. Press second flavor against sides of mold, to cover.
3. Press third flavor of ice cream on top of first flavor on bottom of the mold.
4. Beat whipping cream until stiff, adding sugar gradually. Fold in Marsala wine and brandy. Add glacé fruit and spread over third flavor of ice cream in center of mold.
5. Finally, top with fourth flavor of ice cream, rounding top in a dome shape. Cover and wrap tightly with saran wrap to seal. Freeze 24 hours.
6. To serve, unmold and cut into quarters.

Choose colors and flavors of ice cream for taste and eye appeal.

To unmold, dip mold gently into pan of hot water until there is first evidence *Spumoni* is beginning to release from pan. Quickly turn mold upside down onto edged sheet pan, striking top to release.

Individual servings may be resealed in saran wrap and kept frozen for future use.

Use a light touch when adding sugar, wine and brandy to whipped cream so that cream will reach its ultimate potential and will not separate.

Dinner for Four

Potage Boula Boula

Steak au Poivre, Sauce Béarnaise

*Belgian Endive Salad
with
Mustard Dressing*

*Coconut Cream Heart
with
Fresh Strawberries*

Wine:

Lambert Bridge Cabernet Sauvignon, 1975

*Charlie Ober, Owner/Executive Chef
Michael Werasak, Chef*

The Restaurant of Charlie·O is a perfect extension of its creator, owner and executive chef, Charles Ober. The decor, the ambiance, indeed, the 'personality' of this exciting and energetic establishment is a tribute to Charlie, a talented entrepreneur from Frieburg, Germany. What Pete Rose is to baseball, Charlie Ober is to the restaurant business— 'Charlie Hustle.'

Charles Ober started his apprenticeship in the culinary arts at the famous Casino Restaurant at Konstanz, Germany, and later in Baden-Baden, at the Hotel Storchen in Zurich, the Hilton in Istanbul, the Mid-Ocean Club in Bermuda, and the Four Seasons in New York City before eventually settling in Carmel. His extensive education and experience in both the art of cooking and the business of management covered a period of fourteen years.

In 1973, Charlie and a partner opened the quaint Western Union and General Store Restaurant next to the Forge-In-The-Forest in Carmel. It was very successful, but Charlie needed a solo canvas for his culinary artistry. In 1976, he opened The Restaurant of Charlie · O. The rest is history.

With his wife Melinda, hostess Mary Anne McAbery and chef Michael Werasak from Thailand, Charlie has built "a winner" on a solid foundation of delicious food, which he describes as cosmopolitan, and on friendly and efficient service. "Cosmopolitan is the way people like to eat today." With this combination, Charlie · O doesn't need the lure of hard liquor to fill every table.

Charles Ober has plans for expansion, including restaurants in outer areas, but with all this emphasis on management, he insists, "I always keep my foot in the kitchen."

On Dolores Street, South of Ocean Avenue
Carmel

POTAGE BOULA BOULA

6 tablespoons butter
1 small onion, finely chopped
2 stalks celery, finely chopped
3 cups shelled green peas, or equivalent frozen peas
Salt
Freshly cracked white pepper
1 cup chicken stock
1/4 cup water
1 large can (3 to 4 cups) turtle soup, strained—reserving the meat
6 large oysters
2 tablespoons all-purpose flour
1 cup heavy cream, whipped
Dash each of Madeira and brandy
Garnish: 4 teaspoons whipped cream
            nutmeg

1. Melt butter in a large heavy pan. Add onion and celery. Stir and cook
   2 minutes over low heat. Add peas, a little salt and pepper, chicken
   stock, and water. Stir and mix. Cover and cook over very low heat
   until peas are soft.
2. Remove pan from heat and stir in flour and turtle stock. Stir over
   low heat until mixture comes to a boil. Simmer gently 2 minutes.
3. Purée mixture in an electric blender.
4. Return to pan, place over very low heat and stir in whipped cream,
   reserving 4 teaspoons for garnish. Dice turtle meat and add to soup.
5. Quickly sauté oysters, de-glaze with Madeira and brandy, and add
   to soup.
6. Top each bowl of soup with a teaspoon of whipped cream and place
   under broiler just to glaze.
7. Serve with a sprinkle of nutmeg on top.

STEAK AU POIVRE, SAUCE BEARNAISE

Prepare your *Sauce Béarnaise* in advance.

4 individual steaks, preferably good center-cut shell steaks
1/4 cup butter, melted
1 green pepper
1 red pepper
1/2 can imported Madagascar peppercorns
Few drops brandy
Sauce Béarnaise

1. Beat steaks briefly with side of cleaver to break fibers. Score surface lightly by making a few criss-cross slashes with a knife.
2. Using half of melted butter, brush one side of each steak. Chill in refrigerator to set butter. Repeat on other side of steaks.
3. Cut half or more of each pepper into thin strips, and sauté al dente. Set aside.
4. Preheat griddle, or use sauté pan. Brown one side of steaks over high heat, working with two steaks at a time. Reduce heat to medium and turn steaks; cook to desired degree of doneness. Set aside, keeping warm, and repeat process with remaining steaks.
5. When ready to serve, lace with peppercorns, add brandy, and flame.
6. Arrange steaks on hot serving platter and surround with sautéed pepper strips.
7. Serve with *Sauce Béarnaise.*

SAUCE BEARNAISE

5 egg yolks
1 tablespoon tarragon vinegar
3 tablespoons light cream
1/2 cup frozen sweet butter
1 teaspoon finely chopped white onion or shallot
1/8 teaspoon finely chopped garlic
1 tablespoon chopped fresh parsley
1 teaspoon chopped fresh tarragon, or 1/4 teaspoon dry
1 teaspoon chopped fresh chives
1/4 teaspoon tomato paste
1/8 teaspoon concentrated brown sauce, with Madeira
1 drop lemon juice
1 teaspoon A-1 Sauce

1. Put egg yolks in a small bowl. Beat in vinegar and light cream. Stand
   bowl in a shallow pan, half full of hot water, over low heat. Stir with
   a small whisk until the sauce thickens.
2. Cut frozen sweet butter into small pieces and stir into egg mixture, bit
   by bit. Stir in remaining ingredients.
3. Cover with foil and stand sauce over warm water until ready to use.
   If it becomes too stiff, thin with heavy cream and whip slightly
   a few seconds.

Tip: Sauce Béarnaise cannot successfully be reheated over direct heat.

BELGIAN ENDIVE SALAD WITH MUSTARD DRESSING

2 bunches Belgian endive
Mustard Dressing

1. Wash and dry endive. Refrigerate to crisp.
2. Dress with *Mustard Dressing* and serve on a cold plate.

MUSTARD DRESSING

1 teaspoon Kosher salt or 1/2 teaspoon regular salt
1/2 teaspoon freshly cracked black peppercorns
1/2 teaspoon freshly cracked white peppercorns
1/2 teaspoon granulated sugar
1/2 teaspoon dry mustard
1 teaspoon Dijon mustard
1/2 teaspoon fresh lemon juice
2 tablespoons tarragon vinegar
2 tablespoons pure olive oil
1/2 cup vegetable oil
3 raw egg yolks
1/2 teaspoon finely chopped garlic
1 teaspoon Thai Tiparo Fish Sauce or Chinese Fish Sauce
1 teaspoon Worcestershire
Dash celery salt
Dash Knorr Aromat
Dash fresh herb mixture (Herb Province)
Dash ground bay leaf

1. Put all ingredients into a 1-pint screwtop jar and close tightly. Shake
   very thoroughly.
2. Store in refrigerator up to about two months.

Tip: Special spices can be found in the gourmet section of most groceries.
   If Aromat is not available you may use Lawry Seasoning Salt.

COCONUT CREAM HEART WITH FRESH STRAWBERRIES

1/2 pound fresh cream cheese at room temperature
1/2 cup confectioners' sugar
Pinch salt
1 fresh vanilla bean
4 ounces snow coconut
1/4 cup coconut cream
1 pint heavy cream
1/4 cup dry sherry
3/4 cup red currant jelly
1-1/2 cups fresh strawberries
1 tablespoon lemon juice

1. Combine cream cheese and confectioners' sugar in mixing bowl and beat well. Add a pinch of salt. Slit vanilla bean lengthwise and add half of the seeds.
2. Beat in snow coconut and coconut cream.
3. In a large bowl, whip cream and add to the cream cheese mixture, mixing thoroughly.
4. Cut 4 squares of doubled cheesecloth large enough to line 4 individual heart-shaped molds. Submerge in ice water and wring out. Line molds with cloths.
5. Fill lined molds with cheese mixture, and cover with ends of cloths. Place in refrigerator for 6 hours, or overnight.
6. In a small saucepan, combine sherry and currant jelly and stir over a low fire until jelly melts. Cool and add fresh strawberries coated with lemon juice.

To serve—

Turn each mold upside down on its plate. Holding the cloth, lift up mold and gently peel off cloth. Serve with separate container of strawberry sauce.

Tip: Shredded fresh coconut meat blended with coconut milk may be substituted for snow coconut and coconut cream.

CHEZ FELIX

Dinner for Four

Bisque de Crabe

Salade Printaniere
with
Sauce Vinaigrette

Paupiettes de Sole Normande
Poached in Seafood Sauce

Carottes Sauté à la Vichy

Courgette and Fresh Tomato Provencale

Pommes Fondante

Vacherin Glace Vanille

Wine:

With Entrée: Beaujolais Nouveau or Blanc de Blancs

Felix and Anne Roux, Owners
Felix Roux, Chef

The moment you walk into Chez Felix Restaurant you know you are in for something special and very, very French. No matter what time of day or night, there is always an aroma of something marvelous in the making. The intimate 35-seat dining room is adjacent to chef Roux's small but efficiently laid out kitchen—homey, just like your kitchen or mine. But another reason for the cozy feeling is the wonderful French hospitality of Felix and Anne Roux. They are truly masters of their crafts.

Chef Felix learned his trade from Paul Ripoll, his stepfather, known as the best maker of bouillabaisse on the French Riviera. Later, young Felix served as apprentice under some of Europe's finest chefs and finally came to Carmel, by way of Canada. Felix and Anne worked at different Peninsula restaurants for the first year or so, then opened their own on Cannery Row. It had a magnificent view of Monterey Bay, and Felix became known for his outstanding cuisine. The ambiance, however, could not compare with that of their present location, tucked into a corner of the Sundial Lodge on Monte Verde Street.

A dinner here is like a trip to France—a memorable experience.

In Sundial Lodge, Monte Verde Street at 7th
Carmel

BISQUE DE CRABE

1 large crab, cooked and cleaned
1/4 pound butter
2 carrots, finely diced
1 stalk celery, finely chopped
1 large onion, finely chopped
2 bay leaves
1 sprig fresh thyme, or 3/4 teaspoon dried
1 sprig marjoram, or 3/4 teaspoon dried
1/4 sprig rosemary, or 1/4 teaspoon dried
1/4 cup brandy
6 tablespoons flour
4 cups water
1/4 cup white wine
1 cup thick cream, heated
Sherry
Salt to taste
Dash Spanish saffron
Dash cayenne pepper—optional

1. Remove meat from shell and chop into small pieces. Retain shell and claws.
2. Melt butter in large soup pot. Sauté crabmeat; remove and hold to one side.
3. In the same pot, sauté vegetables and herbs over a low heat until golden. Crush shell and claws and add to pot. Continue cooking for 20 minutes, stirring occasionally.
4. Remove from heat, add 1 tablespoon brandy, and ignite. When flame has extinguished itself, stir briskly. Sprinkle with flour and stir to blend. Continue cooking over low heat for another 15 minutes, stirring occasionally.
5. Pour in water and wine and cook an additional 20 minutes. Strain through a fine sieve and keep hot.
6. When ready to serve, add chopped crabmeat. Heat cream and add to soup. Pour in remaining brandy and a good sherry.
7. Salt to taste. Add a touch of Spanish saffron for color and a touch of cayenne, if desired. Mix well and serve.

SALADE PRINTANIERE WITH SAUCE VINAIGRETTE

We prefer butter lettuce for our *Printaniere*.

Spring salad greens
Sauce Vinaigrette

Prepare greens with care, selecting only the best leaves. Wash, spin-dry and crisp in refrigerator until ready for use.

SAUCE VINAIGRETTE

1/2 cup olive oil
2 tablespoons red wine vinegar
Salt to taste
Fresh ground pepper to taste
1 teaspoon French Dijon mustard

Mix well at the table.

Never let the blade of a knife touch the tender leaves of salad greens. *Tear* the leaves into bite sizes.

PAUPIETTES DE SOLE NORMANDE
POACHED IN SEAFOOD SAUCE

4 large filets of sole, or 8 small ones
2 teaspoons finely chopped green onions—use white section only
1/4 cup white wine
Court Bouillon
1/2 cup thick cream
3 egg yolks, beaten
1/4 cup small shrimp
1/2 cup sliced mushrooms
2 tablespoons butter

1. Sprinkle filets with onions and shape into rolls.
2. Combine wine with *Court Bouillon*. Poach filets slowly for about 15 minutes. Remove and hold to one side.
3. Thicken sauce by combining cream with beaten egg yolks; this is called 'liaison.' Add to bouillon. Return to heat and bring to a boiling point, stirring constantly. Remove.
4. Saute shrimp and mushrooms in butter until mushrooms are tender. Stir into sauce.
5. Arrange poached filets in pan, cover with sauce and place beneath broiler until golden brown.

COURT BOUILLON

1/2 cup finely chopped celery
1/2 cup finely diced carrots
1 onion, finely chopped
2 tablespoons butter
1/4 cup coarsely chopped parsley
1-1/2 tablespoons fresh thyme, or 1/2 teaspoon dried
1 bay leaf
2 whole cloves garlic
1-1/2 teaspoons salt
1-1/2 quarts cold water
1-1/2 to 2 pounds fish heads, fins, bones and tails
1/2 cup dry white wine
6 whole peppercorns

1. Sauté celery, carrots and onions in butter until limp.
2. Add parsley, thyme, bay leaf, garlic and salt to 1-1/2 quarts water in pot.
3. Tie all fish parts into cheesecloth bag; add to pot.
4. Cover pot and cook slowly until broth just comes to boiling point, but do not boil.
5. Reduce heat and remove cover. Add white wine and continue to simmer for 20 minutes. Add peppercorns and keep simmering for an additional 10 minutes.
6. Strain through 2 layers of cheesecloth or through a fine-screened sieve.

CAROTTES SAUTE A LA VICHY

1-1/2 pounds fresh Salinas carrots, sliced on bias or in lengthwise strips
Butter
1/2 cup chicken broth or water
Salt to taste
1 tablespoon finely chopped fresh parsley

1. Glaze carrots in butter. Add chicken broth or water, cover and cook over low heat until nearly done, about 10 minutes.
2. Season, sprinkle with parsley, and serve.

COURGETTE AND FRESH TOMATO PROVENCALE

4 slices tomato
1 zucchini, unpeeled
2 tablespoons olive oil
Salt and pepper
Pinch of fresh thyme

1. Cut each tomato slice in half. Cut zucchini in half lengthwise, then cut each piece across to make 4 pieces. Peel each halfway down and make a cut in the peeled section.
3. Insert 2 half-slices of tomato into each cut made in the zucchini. Place in greased baking dish and sprinkle olive oil, salt, pepper and thyme over all.
4. Bake in 350 degree oven for 10 minutes or until done.

Use only fresh vegetables, not canned or frozen. There is no substitute for the 'fresh' taste.

POMMES FONDANTE

2 pounds potatoes, peeled and cut into olive shapes
Water to cover
Salt
Ground pepper
Butter, lightly browned
Finely chopped fresh parsley

1. Cover shaped potatoes with cold water and parboil 3 minutes. Drain thoroughly.
2. Sauté until golden brown in lightly browned butter. Turn potatoes in pan to brown evenly.
3. Season, sprinkle with parsley and serve.

Tip: Use small to medium Idaho potatoes. Cut each potato in half and pare into shape of large olives.

VACHERIN GLACE VANILLE

4 large scoops vanilla ice cream
Meringue Shells
Raspberry Sauce
2 tablespoons almonds, toasted and slivered
1 teaspoon Cognac or brandy

1. Cover each scoop of ice cream with a *Meringue Shell* and top with *Raspberry Sauce.*
2. Sprinkle almonds over the top and add a touch of Cognac or brandy for flavor.

MERINGUE SHELLS

6 large egg whites, at room temperature
1-1/2 cups superfine granulated sugar
Pinch salt
Butter
Flour

1. Preheat oven to 190 degrees.
2. Add salt to egg whites and whip in blender at medium speed for 3 minutes.
3. Turn to high speed and continue beating. When whites begin to peak, begin adding 1 cup of sugar, a little at a time. Continue beating until whites are very stiff, about 1 minute more. Stop blender.
4. Fold in the remaining sugar by hand.
5. Butter and flour a baking sheet, shaking off any excess flour. Fill pastry bag with meringue mixture. Squeeze onto baking sheet in either plain or fluted shapes, about the size of half of a large egg.
6. Place baking sheet in oven and turn off oven. Bake for 2 hours or more, until meringue is light gold, firm, and comes up easily from pan.
7. Cool completely and store in tightly covered container until ready to use.

Tip: These meringues will save for weeks if tightly covered.

RASPBERRY SAUCE

1 cup raspberry wine
1 teaspoon cornstarch or arrowroot, blended with 1 teaspoon water
1 teaspoon lemon juice
1 cup fresh or frozen raspberries, crushed
1 tablespoon brandy

1. Heat wine over medium heat and thicken with cornstarch mixture. Blend until smooth.
2. Add lemon juice and mix well.
3. Add crushed berries and stir.
4. Remove sauce from heat and finish off with brandy.

Dinner for Six

Drums of Heaven

Willie Lum's Barbecued Pork Cream Soup

Empress Spinach Salad

Szechwan Spiced Beef, Hunan Style

Asparagus

Bananas Flambé

Wines:

With Appetizer & Soup: Château St. Jean Fumé Blanc
With Entrée: Robert Mondavi Napa Gamay

Willie Lum, Owner/Manager
Calvin Leon Yee, Chef

Willie Lum opened his unique restaurant in 1973 and named it China Row because it is situated near the old China Point, an early Chinese village on Cannery Row that existed before the canneries. Built on a rocky promontory, the restaurant has a panoramic view of Monterey Bay as well as exotic interior decor. The entrance is meant to recreate the street atmosphere of Hong Kong. The 'Sadie Thompson Saloon' incorporates the romance of the South Pacific in the early '30's.

But it is in the plush Pagoda Room or the beautiful Lantern Room that the diner samples the wide range of Chinese cuisine produced at China Row under the auspices of Tsao Shen, Chinese God of the Kitchen. The kitchen is now overseen by executive chef, Gerald Peters, but the influence of Willie Lum, himself a master chef skilled in the art of 'houhou' or 'fire-timing,' holds sway. Chef Calvin Yee, a native of Canton, is currently creating some of the best Cantonese, Szechwan, and Mandarin dishes offered anywhere and explains his view of the art of cooking thus: "You have to be more of an artist than a scientist in that each dish is an extension of yourself and a creation of your art."

Devotees of Chinese cuisine enjoy some of the finest of that art at the China Row.

44 Cannery Row
Monterey

DRUMS OF HEAVEN

These are known locally as Willie Lum's Chicken Wings.

18 chicken wings
3 ounces ginger root, grated
1 ounce granulated garlic
1 teaspoon sesame oil
1 teaspoon salt
4 dashes Tabasco
1 ounce brandy
1 egg
Shrimp Batter

1. Wash chicken wings and cut away each tip section.
2. Hold each end of a remaining, jointed wing, and disjoint by bending the elbow; do not separate. Holding fingers tightly around smaller bone, press upward, pushing meat from smaller section right into larger section, giving wing a drumstick appearance. Repeat process with all wings.
3. Combine ginger root, garlic, oil, salt, Tabasco, brandy and egg in a bowl and mix well. Marinate wings in mixture approximately 2 to 4 hours at room temperature.
4. Fold wings into *Shrimp Batter*; deep fry at 360 degrees or until golden brown.

SHRIMP BATTER

1 cup flour
2 eggs
1/2 cup cornstarch
1 tablespoon baking powder
Water

Combine all ingredients. Thin with water until the consistency is that of pancake batter. For fluffier batter, add 1 teaspoon oil and 4 ounces beer.

WILLIE LUM'S BARBECUED PORK CREAM SOUP

1/2 cup butter
1/2 cup flour
1/2 pound ground barbecued pork
1/4 teaspoon M.S.G.—optional
2 teaspoons Worcestershire sauce
1 teaspoon Tabasco sauce
2 teaspoons salt
1 teaspoon white pepper
2 cups chicken broth or consomme'
1 quart whole milk
4 tablespoons Madeira
Garnish: barbecued pork strips
          green onions, chopped

1. Melt butter in a large saucepan over low heat. Add ground barbecued pork and mix together.
2. Add flour and stir constantly for 4 to 5 minutes, but do not allow to burn.
3. Add all seasonings to broth and then slowly add to first mixture.
4. Slowly add milk and stir until blended. Let simmer 7 to 10 minutes, stirring constantly.
5. Just before serving, stir in Madeira. Serve garnished with barbecued pork strips, fresh green onion bits and a splash of Madeira.

EMPRESS SPINACH SALAD

1-1/2 pounds fresh spinach, uncooked
2 pimentos, drained and diced
2 slices bacon, crisp-cooked, finely chopped—reserve bacon fat
    for dressing
2 eggs, hard-cooked and chopped
1/4 cup olive oil
3 tablespoons wine vinegar
Pinch salt
Pinch pepper, fresh ground
1 clove garlic, mashed
3 anchovy filets, minced or mashed
Juice of half lemon

1. Wash spinach carefully several times to get rid of all sand. Or buy pre-washed and trimmed fresh spinach, give it a quick wash, and dry well.
2. Place spinach in a bowl, add pimentos, bacon and eggs.
3. Combine oil and vinegar in second bowl. Add salt, pepper, garlic, anchovies and lemon juice. Mix well. When ready to serve, discard bits of garlic; pour dressing and warm bacon grease together and stir until blended.
4. Pour over spinach, toss well and serve.

SZECHWAN SPICED BEEF SHRED, HUNAN STYLE

1 pound flank steak
Marinade
1/4 cup oil
1 teaspoon minced fresh ginger root
2 teaspoons minced garlic
3 scallions, cut 1 inch long—use stems
2 dry red chili peppers, finely ground—use seeds
1 tablespoon pale dry sherry
1 tablespoon Chinese red wine vinegar or cider vinegar
1 teaspoon M.S.G.—optional
6 water chestnuts, coarsely chopped
1 cup shredded bamboo shoots
1/2 green bell pepper, thinly sliced
1/2 cup water or clear chicken broth
2 tablespoons cornstarch, mixed with 1 tablespoon water
1 teaspoon sesame oil

1. Thinly slice steak against the grain, and cut into matchstick-size strips. Marinate for 2 to 4 hours.
2. Heat 4 teaspoons oil in wok to 350 degrees. Add beef mixture and stir to separate pieces. Blanch briskly until beef just loses its redness. Remove to a bowl.
3. Heat 2 tablespoons oil in wok. Add ginger, garlic, scallions and chili peppers. Stir-fry about 10 seconds.
4. Stir in sherry, vinegar and—if desired—M.S.G. Cook until it bubbles gently.
5. Add water chestnuts, bamboo shoots and green bell pepper.
6. Return beef mixture to wok and blend all together.
7. Pour in water or chicken broth. When it begins to boil, stir in cornstarch mixture and continue stirring until sauce thickens.
8. Add sesame oil, mix well and serve.

MARINADE

1/4 teaspoon salt
1/2 teaspoon sugar
1 tablespoon cornstarch

Mix with sliced flank steak, marinate 2 to 4 hours. Cook with beef in Step 2 of recipe.

ASPARAGUS

1-1/2 pounds asparagus
3/4 teaspoon salt
1/2 teaspoon sugar
1/4 teaspoon soy sauce
Few drops sesame oil

1. Snap off tender tips of asparagus and discard the rest. Stems will naturally break where tender part begins. Cut tips diagonally into pieces about 2 1/2 inches long.
2. Boil tips in large saucepan for 2 to 3 minutes. Drain, rinse in cold water and drain again.
3. Sprinkle with salt, sugar, soy sauce and sesame oil. Stir to blend seasonings.
4. Refrigerate in covered container. When chilled, taste again and adjust seasoning if necessary.
5. Serve cold.

BANANAS FLAMBE

Caution is the rule whenever liquors are ignited. Flames beneath pan must be low—or the pan removed from flame entirely—to protect against accidents.

6 tablespoons butter
3/4 cup brown sugar
6 bananas, peeled and sliced lengthwise
1 tablespoon cinnamon
3 ounces banana liqueur
6 ounces white rum
Vanilla ice cream

1. Melt butter in chafing dish. Add brown sugar and blend well.
2. Add bananas and sauté lightly. Sprinkle with cinnamon and lower flame.
3. Pour rum and banana liqueur over bananas. Ignite carefully, basting bananas with flaming liquid.
4. Serve over ice cream when flame dies out.

Tip: Bananas must be ripe for this recipe.

CLAM BOX RESTAURANT

Dinner for Four

Stuffed Baked Clams

Vegetable Soup

*Tossed Salad
with
Italian Dressing*

*Baked Salmon
with
Caper Sauce*

Baked Rice

*Green Beans
with
Garlic*

*Creamed Pie
with
Fresh Fruit or Berries*

Wine:

With Entrée: Paul Masson Pinot Chardonnay

*Clyde and Genevieve Herr, Owners
David Eagle, Manager
Henry Phillips, Chef*

"When in Rome . . ." the saying goes—a sure-fire formula for locating a fine restaurant is to follow the locals. In Carmel that maxim could easily lead the visitor to The Clam Box, tucked away on Mission Street. As the name implies, seafood is a specialty in this cozy, family-owned restaurant. The quality of food and service is a Carmel tradition.

The consistently high quality of the cuisine is due to the talent of chef Henry Phillips, who has been in charge of the kitchen since The Clam Box opened its doors early in the 1960's. Whether the seafood is fresh from Monterey Bay or is flown in from other waters, chef Phillips prepares it in wondrous ways.

The simple, semi-colonial decor is highlighted by a warm, cheery fire. Since Clyde and Genevieve Herr took over the Clam Box in the early 1970's, it is possible to precede your favorite dish with a cocktail. No reservations are accepted, but don't be discouraged if there are other hungry people waiting in the tiny foyer; a meal at The Clam Box is worth the wait.

Mission and Fifth
Carmel

STUFFED BAKED CLAMS

1 white onion
2 teaspoons melted butter
1 teaspoon olive oil
1 stalk celery
5 sprigs fresh parsley
5 fresh mushrooms
1 small can minced clams
12 fresh clams, steamed—reserve shells
1/4 cup sherry
1/4 cup evaporated milk
1 tablespoon Worcestershire
Dash each of the following: curry, thyme, oregano,
   sweet basil, garlic, cumin, Tabasco
1/4 cup cornstarch
1/4 cup cold water
A little melted butter
Parmesan cheese
Paprika

1. Preheat oven to 350 degrees.
2. Finely chop half of onion, reserving other half.
3. Sauté chopped onion in butter mixed with olive oil.
4. Grind together remaining onion, celery, parsley and mushrooms. Add to sautéed onion and continue cooking until moisture is gone.
5. Add all of the clams, sherry and evaporated milk. Add seasonings and, again, continue cooking until moisture is gone.
6. Thicken with cornstarch mixed with cold water. Cook an additional 2 to 3 minutes. Remove from flame and cool.
7. Stuff clam shells. Cover with a little melted butter, Parmesan cheese and paprika.
8. Bake in preheated oven for 20 minutes.

VEGETABLE SOUP

1 small onion, chopped
2 carrots, chopped
1 zucchini, chopped
1 small potato, chopped
2 stalks of celery, chopped
1 small can stewed tomatoes, chopped
1-1/2 quarts chicken broth
Seasoning to taste

Combine vegetables with chicken broth, bring to a boil. Lower flame and simmer 1 to 1-1/2 hours. Add salt and pepper to taste.

TOSSED SALAD WITH ITALIAN DRESSING

Select seasonally available salad greens. Wash, dry and crisp in refrigerator. Serve with *Italian Dressing.*

ITALIAN DRESSING

1/8 teaspoon thyme
1/8 teaspoon cumin
1/4 teaspoon oregano
1/4 teaspoon sweet basil
2 cloves garlic
1 pinch each of nutmeg, curry, rosemary, dry mustard
2 tablespoons catsup
1/2 cup mayonnaise
1/3 cup red wine vinegar
2/3 cup salad oil

Combine and blend until well-mixed.

BAKED SALMON WITH CAPER SAUCE

1 cup water
1/4 onion, sliced
1 stalk celery, shredded
Salt and pepper to taste
2 to 3 slices lemon
4 6- to 8-ounce salmon steaks
2 tablespoons butter
3 tablespoons flour
1 cup fish broth—reserved from poaching
1 cup light cream
1/4 cup white wine—optional
Dash Worcestershire
Salt and pepper to taste
Garnish: capers

1. Bring water, onion, celery, salt, pepper and lemon slices to a boil. Cook rapidly for 5 minutes.
2. Reduce heat. Add salmon steaks and poach for 8 minutes. Remove salmon to a buttered baking dish and keep warm. Reserve liquid.
3. Cook butter and flour together to form a roux, but *do not brown.* Add reserved poaching liquid and cream. Whisk together rapidly to prevent lumps. Add wine if desired, but do not boil once wine has been added. Add Worcestershire, salt and pepper to taste.
4. Pour sauce over fish and sprinkle with capers.
5. Bake in 350 degree oven for 15 minutes.

BAKED RICE

1 tablespoon finely chopped onion
3/4 cup raw rice
2 tablespoons butter
3-1/4 cups water

1. Preheat oven to 350 degrees.
2. Sauté onion and rice in butter. Add water.
3. Transfer rice to baking dish and bake in preheated oven 20 minutes, covered.

GREEN BEANS WITH GARLIC

1 garlic clove, minced
4 tablespoons butter
1 pound fresh green beans

1. Sauté garlic in butter and add green beans. Cover.
2. Continue cooking until beans are just tender. Stir occasionally to prevent sticking. Moisture from vegetables should be enough, but if you need more, add only one or two tablespoons of water.

Clam Box

CREAMED PIE WITH FRESH FRUIT OR BERRIES

3 ounces cream cheese
1 teaspoon unflavored gelatin, softened in 1 teaspoon cold water
1/3 teaspoon vanilla
1/3 cup sugar
1 pint whipping cream
1 baked pie shell or graham cracker crust

1. Cream together cream cheese, gelatin, vanilla and sugar in mixer, scraping sides as you mix.
2. Add whipping cream and beat rapidly until stiff, but do not overbeat.
3. Put in pie shell and freeze 1 hour.
4. Serve topped with fresh fruit or berries in season.

Dinner for Four

Scallops Scituate

Greek Lemon Soup

Artichoke Abrego

Castroville Chicken Caldrone

Broccoli with Lemon/Dill Butter

California Fruit and Cheese

Coffee

Wines:

With Appetizer, Soup & Salad: Oakville Napa Fumé, 1976
With Entrée & Dessert: Enz Late Harvest Pinot St. George, 1974
After Dinner: Grand Marnier

Eddie Winstead & Hal Evans, Owners
Mike McIntyre, Executive Chef

Back in 1954, the late Vic Knight created an indoor-outdoor eatery from an old garage, originally part of the Abrego Adobe located across the street. Not being sure the venture would succeed, he didn't put his name on it. He called it 'Rings,' for reasons known only to himself, wrote the menu on a chalkboard hanging over the open kitchen area, and commenced a series of hilariously far-out ads in the local newspapers. Rings had no cash register; no one got a check. Vic trusted everyone to report what he had eaten for lunch and to pay for it; practically everyone did! As proclaimed by a sign at the entrance of his walled patio, Rings was 'Under No Management.' Rings became a Monterey institution, and people loved it. In 1968, Vic Knight retired.

Bob Canon, Blaine McDonough, Jim Stone and Harrison Thompson then leased the location, installed a large antique 'jewelers-clock' sign they had found and renamed the restaurant The Clock. Later, they converted the patio into a lovely garden dining area, and changed the name again, this time to The Clock Garden Restaurant. Eddie Winstead and Hal Evans have since acquired ownership. Eddie and Hal have a solid background in the restaurant business here on the Monterey Peninsula and know what Montereyans want. They solemnly promise "not to tamper with the success of one of the most popular restaurants in the area . . . it will still be The Clock . . . the same Clock."

Top-notch chef Mike McIntyre describes his cuisine as Californian because he features local meats, fish and produce as well as an exclusively California wine list. Casually elegant, the Clock Garden Restaurant may be a long way from the old 'Under No Management' Rings, but people still love it.

565 Abrego
Monterey

SCALLOPS SCITUATE

2 shallots
1 clove garlic
2-1/2 tablespoons butter
1 pound fresh scallops
1/3 teaspoon salt
1/4 teaspoon white pepper
1/2 cup sauterne
3/4 pound mushrooms, sliced
1 to 1-1/2 tablespoons lemon juice
1 tablespoon flour
Garnish: 1 tablespoon finely chopped parsley
              lemon wedges or slices

1. Finely chop shallots and garlic and sauté in 1 tablespoon butter until golden, but not brown.
2. Add scallops, sprinkle with salt and pepper and sauté for 4 minutes—*no more*—turning once. Add sauterne and simmer for an additional 4 minutes. Remove scallops and set aside.
3. Add mushrooms and lemon juice to pan. Simmer gently until mushrooms are just limp. Turn off heat.
4. In a separate small pan, make a roux of the flour and remaining butter. Do not let the roux brown, but cook it thoroughly to remove taste of flour.
5. Re-light heat beneath sauce/mushroom mixture. Add roux and mix thoroughly. Cook gently until sauce is slightly thickened.
6. Return scallops to pan, add chopped parsley, and mix gently.
7. Serve immediately, garnishing with a little additional chopped parsley and wedges or slices of lemon.

GREEK LEMON SOUP

1 small chicken
1 carrot, coarsely chopped
1 stalk celery, coarsely chopped
1 small onion, coarsely chopped
2 bay leaves
2 tablespoons chicken soup base
2 quarts cold water
1-1/2 cups sauterne—reserve 1/2 cup for later use
1/2 teaspoon salt
1/2 teaspoon white pepper
1/2 cup rice
4 tablespoons butter
2 egg yolks
2 tablespoons lemon juice
Garnish: 4 thin slices lemon
                1 tablespoon finely chopped parsley

1. Combine first 10 ingredients in large stock pot and bring to a boil. Reduce heat to simmer and cook gently 2 to 3 hours, or until chicken falls from bones.
2. Strain broth. Discard vegetables but reserve chicken. Chill broth until fat can easily be skimmed from the top.
3. Transfer 1 quart broth to another soup kettle. Remove chicken from carcass and chop into fine dice.
4. Bring broth to a boil and add rice. Simmer 20 to 30 minutes, or until rice is cooked. Add diced chicken 5 minutes before rice is done.
5. Add butter and reserved sauterne. Keep soup over low heat.
6. In a small bowl, beat together egg yolks and lemon juice until frothy.
7. Add 1 cup hot soup to egg mixture. Return the entire mixture to soup kettle, mixing gently but thoroughly.
8. Serve immediately, garnishing each bowl with a lemon slice and a sprinkle of chopped parsley.

ARTICHOKE ABREGO

2 large artichokes
1 tablespoon olive oil
1 tablespoon white wine vinegar
2 teaspoons salt
2 stalks celery, chopped
1/2 teaspoon white pepper
2 bay leaves
2-1/2 cups boiling water
Artichoke Sauce
Garnish: Parsley or watercress sprigs

1. Trim 3/4 inch to 1 inch from top of artichokes. Trim stem back to base and remove small leaves around the bottom. Split artichokes in half lengthwise. Put halves together and place, bottoms down, in a pot small enough for artichokes to remain standing.
2. Add oil, vinegar, salt, chopped celery, garlic, pepper and bay leaves. Pour boiling water over all, cover pot and bring to a full boil for 10 minutes. Reduce heat and simmer for 15 minutes more.
3. Remove artichokes and drain face-down on paper towels. Cool.
4. With a sharp-edged silver teaspoon or similar instrument, remove prickly purple-green leaves in the center, and remove 'choke.' Chill artichokes.

To serve—

Place one half artichoke per serving face down on salad plate. Spoon 2 tablespoons of *Artichoke Sauce* onto plate to one side of artichoke. Garnish with parsley or watercress.

ARTICHOKE SAUCE

1 cup homemade or high quality mayonnaise
1/2 cup sour cream
1/2 teaspoon salt
1/4 teaspoon white pepper
1/4 teaspoon garlic powder
2 teaspoons dry mustard
1-1/2 to 2 tablespoons lemon juice, depending on tartness desired

Whisk together until well blended.

Tip: You may use any high quality mayonnaise—we use Best Foods—if you don't want to make your own from scratch.

CASTROVILLE CHICKEN CALDRONE

2 chicken breasts, boned and skinned
4 chicken legs, skinned
4 chicken thighs, skinned
2 large or 3 small shallots, finely chopped
2 small cloves garlic, finely chopped
1/2 cup butter, melted
1/4 teaspoon saffron
1/2 cup brandy
3/4 pound mushrooms, sliced
1-1/3 cups Madeira
8 whole mushrooms
6 ounces quartered artichoke hearts, packed in brine
2 ounces artichoke heart brine
2/3 cup light cream—half-and-half is fine
2/3 cup whipping cream
1 tablespoon chicken soup base or chicken bouillon
1/3 teaspoon salt
1/2 teaspoon white pepper
1 tablespoon Worcestershire
1 to 2 tablespoons roux
4 whole artichoke hearts

1. Cut chicken breasts in half and dry all chicken thoroughly on paper towels.
2. In sauté pan, sauté shallots and garlic in 2 tablespoons melted butter until golden but not brown. Add chicken pieces and sprinkle with saffron. Sauté over low heat for 15 minutes on 1 side and 10 minutes on the other.
3. Flame with brandy.
4. Put 1 half-breast, 1 thigh and 1 leg in each of 4 individual deep casseroles, with covers.
5. Sauté sliced mushrooms in sauté pan, adding a bit more melted butter if needed. Add 2/3 cup Madeira and sauté 5 minutes more. With slotted spoon, divide mushrooms evenly over chicken in casseroles. Strain remaining liquid in sauté pan into a heavy 2 or 3 quart saucepan.

6. In the same chicken/mushroom saute pan, saute whole mushrooms on both sides in a little butter until golden brown. Set aside.

7. Make roux with 3 tablespoons flour blended into 3 tablespoons melted butter, cooking 5 minutes to eliminate taste of flour; do not let the roux brown. Set aside.

8. Purée artichoke heart-quarters and brine thoroughly in blender. Add to saucepan with mushroom liquid. Add light cream, whipping cream, remaining Madeira, chicken soup base, salt, pepper and Worcestershire. Simmer gently over low heat, whisking in roux until sauce is creamy and slightly thick.

9. Divide sauce evenly over chicken, using approximately 1 cup per casserole. Cut the whole artichoke hearts in half, allowing 2 halves per serving. Add artichoke halves and 2 whole mushrooms to each casserole. Cover pots and cook in 350 degree oven for 35 minutes.

10. Serve with *Steamed Rice.*

To serve—

Spoon out chicken and sauce onto plate, at table.

STEAMED RICE

1 cup long grain rice
2 1/2 cups boiling water
1 tablespoon butter
1/2 teaspoon salt

1. Stir rice into boiling water. Add butter and salt. Cover.
2. Lower heat and simmer for 1/2 hour, until rice takes up all liquid.
3. Fluff, and serve.

BROCCOLI WITH LEMON/DILL BUTTER

1 bunch broccoli
2 teaspoons salt
4 tablespoons butter
1-1/2 teaspoons dill weed
2 tablespoons lemon juice

1. Trim broccoli and cut into serving spears. Cover with cold water, add salt, and bring to a boil. Reduce heat and simmer for approximately 12 minutes or until just tender but still quite firm.
2. Plunge broccoli into cold water for 5 minutes to stop cooking and to retain green color. Drain on paper towels and place in oven-proof pie plate or other low rimmed pan.
3. About 15 minutes before serving, place broccoli in 350 degree oven to reheat.
4. Meantime, melt butter over low heat and add dill and lemon juice.
5. To serve, spoon lemon/dill butter over spears arranged on plates.

Lemon juice is a superb flavor enhancer, as well as having a wonderful flavor of its own. We use it a lot in our recipes.

CALIFORNIA FRUIT AND CHEESE

4 green Pippin apples or green ripe pears
4 3-ounce wedges Rouge et Noir Brie
16 to 20 Carr table water biscuits

1. About 3 hours before serving, remove Brie from refrigerator to soften.
2. Serve on dessert plate with a whole apple or pear, and 4 or 5
   table water biscuits.

CLUB XIX

Dinner for Four

Lobster Bisque

Rack of Lamb

Green Peas au Naturel

Boulangere Potatoes

Sliced Tomato Salad

Soufflé au Grand Marnier

Wines:

Aperitif: Albert Pic et Fils Chablis Grand Cru "Vaudésir"
With Entrée: Silver Oak Cabernet Sauvignon, 1974
With Dessert: Schramsberg Blanc de Blancs

Pierre Bain, Manager/Maître d'
Jean Louis Tourel, Executive Chef
P. De La Cruz, Chef

Club XIX is on the ground floor of The Lodge at Pebble Beach, facing the Pacific. It seats about fifty diners in its elegant interior, and another thirty or forty on its lovely dining terrace, beyond the sliding glass doors. The interior decor is of handsome wood paneling and leather. One wall is a subtly lit wine rack, another a well-stocked bar with a regal brass espresso coffee machine. A third glass wall looks across the entrance way at a colorful gallery of 18th Century Scottish and English golfers. But it is the exterior wall of glass, looking over the terrace to one of nature's true spectacles, Carmel Bay, Point Lobos and the most beautiful 18th hole in golfdom—the famous 'finishing hole at Pebble,' that sets this restaurant so high on the list of special places to visit on the Monterey Peninsula.

Pierre Bain, the manager and maitre d', is a fortunate man to be surrounded by such beauty every day. "What is unique about our restaurant? Our cuisine and our view!" he says proudly. Pierre received his training at the famous Hotel School in Nice, France. His career took him to the Mid-Ocean Club in Bermuda and the Etoile in San Francisco before he finally came to Monterey Peninsula in 1966 for the opening of Club XIX. Since 1969 he has been its gracious maitre d' and manager.

Under the watchful eye of executive chef de cuisine, Jean Jouis Tourel, Club XIX and its talented crew have won culinary awards year after year.

The Lodge at Pebble Beach, 17 Mile Drive
Pebble Beach

LOBSTER BISQUE

1 medium-sized boiled lobster
Lobster shells and tough ends of claws
Coral roe if available
2-1/2 cups fish stock
1 onion, sliced
2 ribs celery, with leaves
2 whole cloves
1 bay leaf
6 peppercorns, crushed
1/4 cup butter
1/4 cup flour
2 cups milk, heated
Dash nutmeg
1 cup cream, hot but not boiling
Salt and pepper to taste
1 ounce brandy

1. Remove meat from lobster. Dice body meat, and mince tail and claw meat. Reserve.
2. Crush shells, add claws and combine with fish stock, onion, celery, cloves, bay leaf and peppercorns. If there is coral roe available, force through a fine sieve into same pot.
3. Simmer 30 minutes and strain stock.
4. Make roux of flour and butter. Gradually add milk. Add dash of nutmeg.
5. When sauce is smooth and simmering, add lobster and fish stock. Cover and simmer 5 minutes. Turn off heat.
6. Stir in hot cream and season to taste.
7. Add brandy and serve at once.

RACK OF LAMB

1 rack of young lamb—allow for 8 chops
1 garlic clove, cut open
Thyme
Butter
Salt and pepper
Sauce Hollandaise with Fresh Mint

1. Preheat oven to 400 degrees.
2. Remove fell (membrane) and excess fat from lamb.
3. Rub all over with garlic. Coat with thyme, butter, salt and pepper. Place on metal rack in shallow pan. Roast for about 25 minutes, until internal temperature reaches 145 degrees on meat thermometer.
4. Serve with *Sauce Hollandaise with Fresh Mint.*

Tip: If you French the rib bones, cover the tips with foil.

SAUCE HOLLANDAISE WITH FRESH MINT

3 large egg yolks
2 tablespoons cold water
1 stick butter
2 teaspoons lemon juice
2 teaspoons chopped fresh mint
Pinch cayenne

1. Combine egg yolks and water in saucepan.
2. In separate pan, melt butter. Remove from heat.
3. Heat egg yolks and water over very low heat. Beat with a whisk 2 or 3 minutes until yolks are thick and pale yellow.
4. Add 2 tablespoons of the butter, warm but not hot, and continue beating. Remove pan from heat.
5. Continue adding butter in small amounts until all is used, beating constantly.
6. Return pan to low heat. Add lemon juice, mint and cayenne, and beat a little longer until sauce is well blended and glossy. It should stand in peaks.
7. Set pan in bowl of warm water until ready to serve. Beat 30 seconds before spooning into serving bowl.

BLENDER HOLLANDAISE

1 stick butter
3 large egg yolks
1 tablespoon lemon juice
Pinch cayenne
2 teaspoons chopped fresh mint

1. In a small heavy saucepan, melt butter over low heat. Remove.
2. Combine egg yolks, lemon juice and cayenne in blender. Cover blender and switch on and off quickly several times.
3. Remove cover, turn to high speed and gradually pour in warm melted butter.
4. Cover blender. Blend for 1 minute, then turn off for 1/2 minute. Repeat 10 to 12 times until sauce thickens and peaks.
5. Add mint, blend again and serve.

GREEN PEAS AU NATUREL

1 pound fresh green peas
Water or light chicken stock, boiling
1/2 teaspoon lemon juice
Pinch sugar
2 or 3 pea pods
Melted butter, or hot cream
Salt and pepper to taste
Sprinkle of chopped parsley or fresh oregano—optional

1. Pour enough boiling water or chicken stock over peas to cover. Add lemon juice, sugar and pea pods for flavor. Simmer 7 to 10 minutes. When peas are tender, drain. Remove pods.
2. Season with butter or cream. Salt and pepper to taste. Chopped parsley or fresh oregano may be added if desired. Stir together and serve.

POTATOES BOULANGERE

4 medium-large potatoes, peeled and sliced
Butter
2 medium onions, sliced
2 bay leaves
1-1/2 teaspoons thyme
Beef stock
Salt and freshly ground black pepper to taste
Finely chopped parsley

1. Preheat oven to 380 to 400 degrees.
2. Saute sliced potatoes in butter over medium heat until golden. Remove potatoes and saute onions in remaining fat until golden.
3. Return potatoes to pan and add beef stock to cover.
4. Season with salt and pepper. Add bay leaves and thyme.
5. Bake for 25 minutes in preheated oven until golden brown.
6. Sprinkle with parsley and serve.

SLICED TOMATO SALAD

4 tomatoes, peeled and thinly sliced
1 small white onion, thinly sliced
Salt
Lettuce leaves
2 tablespoons finely chopped fresh parsley
Black pepper, freshly ground
Pinch leaf oregano—optional
Vinaigrette Dressing à la Pierre

1. Sprinkle tomatoes and onions with salt. Refrigerate in glass or enamel pan until very cold.
2. Arrange on lettuce; sprinkle with parsley and pepper. Top with oregano if desired.
3. Dress with *Vinaigrette à la Pierre* and serve.

Pre-salting the tomatoes and onions and allowing them to 'rest' brings forth their flavor.

VINAIGRETTE DRESSING A LA PIERRE

1-1/4 cups oil
1/4 cup vinegar
1/2 teaspoon salt

Mix all ingredients well. This makes 1-1/2 cups.

***Using five parts of oil to one of vinegar—rather than the standard
three-to-one ratio—is what makes our vinaigrette so special.***

SOUFFLE AU GRAND MARNIER

Butter for mold
Sugar for mold
2-1/2 tablespoons butter
3 tablespoons flour
1 cup milk
1/4 cup sugar
4 egg yolks
1/4 cup Grand Marnier
1 teaspoon vanilla
6 egg whites
Pinch salt
1/8 teaspoon cream of tartar
3 tablespoons powdered sugar, sifted

1. Preheat oven to 400 degrees.
2. Butter and sugar a 1-1/2 quart soufflé dish or straight-sided mold.
3. Melt butter in a heavy saucepan. Add flour and cook, stirring, for
   1 or 2 minutes. Add milk gradually, beating with a wire whisk.
4. Add sugar and cook several minutes to form a thick sauce. Remove
   pan from heat.
5. Beat in egg yolks one at a time. Add Grand Marnier and vanilla.
6. Beat egg whites with salt. Add cream of tartar and continue
   beating until stiff peaks form. Stir 1/4 of the egg whites into yolk
   mixture, then carefully fold in remainder.
7. Place in dish and bake in preheated oven 10 minutes. Lower heat to
   350 degrees and continue baking 20 minutes more, until soufflé
   is puffed and golden.
8. Sprinkle with powdered sugar and serve immediately.

Dinner for Four

Covey's Nest

Soupe à l'Oignon Gratinée

Escalopes de Veau du Chef

Fresh Spinach Maison

Tarte Tatin

Wines:

With Appetizer: Mirassou Gewurtztraminer, 1977
With Entrée: Robert Mondavi Napa Gamay, 1977

Csaba Ajan, Manager
Charles Lee, Chef

Only eight hotels in the United States were outstanding enough in 1979 to receive the 5-Star Award from the Mobil Travel Guide. One of these was the Quail Lodge at Carmel Valley Golf and Country Club. It is most fitting to find there another of the fine Monterey Peninsula restaurants, appropriately called The Covey. Situated alongside a beautiful waterhole where both native and migratory birds congregate, it is a lovely place noted for its country sophistication.

Both the Lodge and The Covey are under the aegis of Mr. Hoby Hooker. He is rightfully enthusiastic about the talents of maître d' Michael Revicky and chef Charles Lee. The service is most competent and gracious— and, since a restaurant's reputation rests primarily on the shoulders of its chef, it should be noted that chef Lee carries his burden well.

Dining areas, done in pewter and fine woods, are partitioned in such a way as to give maximum privacy, creating a pleasant, restful ambiance.

Edgar Haber, president of Green Meadows, Inc.—the developer of the Golf Club, Quail Lodge and The Covey—has made a real contribution to the preservation of the beauty of Carmel Valley.

Carmel Valley Road
Carmel

COVEY'S NEST

4 medium tomatoes, cored
1 head butter, leaf or red lettuce
1/2 pound small Bay shrimp
Garnish: 4 lemon wedges
               olives—optional
               chopped parsley—optional
               paprika—optional

Dressing

1. Cut tomatoes into star arrangement. Place on bed of lettuce.
2. Fill tomato cavities with equal portions of shrimp. Garnish with
   lemon, olives, parsley, and paprika as desired.
3. Serve with *Dressing.*

DRESSING

1 tablespoon dry mustard
2 tablespoons Worcestershire
6 anchovy filets, chopped
1 uncooked egg
1/2 clove garlic, minced
1 cup oil
2 tablespoons red wine vinegar
Juice of 1 lemon

Mix all ingredients well.

We also use this dressing for our Caesar's Salad at The Covey.

SOUPE A L'OIGNON GRATINEE

6 onions
1/2 pound butter
3 tablespoons flour
1 cup white wine
4 cups beef stock
1 bay leaf
Salt
White pepper
4 slices sourdough French bread
Butter
Parmesan cheese, grated
Paprika
4 slices Swiss cheese

1. Saute' sliced onions in butter. Add flour and white wine. Blend well.
2. Add stock and bay leaf. Season with salt and pepper to taste. Simmer slowly for 3 hours.
3. When ready to serve, fill individual ovenproof bowls.
4. Preheat oven to 350 degrees.
5. Butter bread slices and sprinkle with Parmesan cheese and paprika. Bake in preheated oven until golden brown.
6. Top each bowl with toast and a slice of Swiss cheese. Broil until cheese melts. Serve piping hot.

Tip: Season with a light hand—as the broth reduces, seasoning becomes more apparent.

ESCALOPES DE VEAU DU CHEF

1-1/2 pounds Provimi milk-fed veal loin, trimmed and sliced into
    2-ounce cutlets
Salt
White pepper
Clarified butter
Juice of 1 fresh lemon
4 medium shallots, finely chopped
1/4 pound butter, softened
1 tablespoon finely chopped fresh parsley
12 thin slices lemon

1. Pound cutlets with flat side of meat mallet until uniformly thin.
2. Season with salt and pepper. Saute' in clarified butter, and hold on
   hot plate.
3. Using same pan at low heat, add softened—not melted—butter, lemon
   juice, shallots and parsley. Add veal and allow to simmer for 2 to 3
   minutes over low heat.
4. Remove veal and arrange on serving plates with slice of lemon
   between each cutlet.
5. Pour remaining sauce over portions and serve.

FRESH SPINACH MAISON

2 bunches crisp fresh spinach
3/4 cup cubed Canadian bacon
2 cloves garlic, finely chopped
1/2 teaspoon dry English mustard
4 tablespoons Worcestershire
2 dashes Tabasco
5 tablespoons brown sugar
1/3 cup malt vinegar
1/4 cup Cognac
Salt
Pepper, freshly ground

1. Wash and stem spinach leaves, towel dry and set aside in a large salad bowl.
2. Fry bacon in saucepan until cubes are semi-crisp. Retain bacon fat. Add garlic, mustard, Worcestershire, Tabasco and sugar. Blend well with wooden spoon over medium heat.
3. Add vinegar and keep blending the dressing until it comes to a boil. Remove from heat.
4. Pour liquid over spinach leaves, holding bacon back in saucepan. Toss leaves with dressing. Place spinach on warm salad plates.
5. Add Cognac to bacon bits in saucepan. Flame bacon with Cognac and sprinkle flamed bacon bits over the spinach.
6. Add salt and pepper to taste.

Tip: Let the flame die completely before adding bacon bits to salad.

TARTE TATIN

Prepare your *Pastry Dough* one day in advance.

2 tablespoons butter
2 cups sugar
4 medium red apples, peeled, cut into wedges, and sprinkled with lemon juice
Cinnamon
1 sheet *Pastry Dough*, 10" diameter
Flavored Whipped Cream

1. Preheat oven to 375 degrees.
2. Melt butter in bottom of pan, sprinkle with a little of the sugar.
3. Arrange prepared apples in a circular pattern; sprinkle with remaining sugar and cinnamon. Top with thin layer of *Pastry Dough*.
4. Cover pan with aluminum foil and place in preheated oven for 20 to 25 minutes.
5. Remove foil and bake until golden brown, from 5 to 15 more minutes.
6. Flip from pan onto serving dish; apples will now be on top.
7. Cut into wedges to serve, topped with *Flavored Whipped Cream*.

PASTRY DOUGH

2 cups flour, sifted
1 tablespoon light brown sugar
1 teaspoon salt
1 teaspoon grated lemon peel
1 cup butter
1 tablespoon milk
1 egg, plus 1 egg yolk, beaten well
1 teaspoon vanilla

1. Place flour on table or in a bowl. Make a well in the middle, and fill with sugar, salt and lemon peel. Blend together.
2. Add butter and mix with hands until all the flour is incorporated.
3. Mix together milk, eggs and vanilla. Add to blended ingredients. Continue mixing until a ball is formed.
4. Cover and refrigerate overnight.
5. When ready to use, roll out to a 10" diameter and use as directed.

FLAVORED WHIPPED CREAM

1/2 pint whipping cream
2 tablespoons powdered sugar
Dash vanilla extract
Dash crème de cacao

Whip cream until stiff. Continue to beat slowly, adding sugar, vanilla and crème de cacao just until blended.

Cypress Room

ALEXANDRE DUMAS (PÉRE)
INVITES YOU TO THE FEAST OF NOEL
FOR FOUR

*Crème de Tortue à l'Extase du Roi Poseidon, Garni de Crevettes
Moules, et Palourdes**

*Saumon à la Chambord du Château Monte Cristo,
avec Champignons Tournés,
Pâté de Marcassin, Quenelles de Saumon
et Sauce Genevoise**

*Mousse Fouettee au jus d'Ananas
Croûte aux Campignons et aux Truffes Noires
à la Bechamel*

*Buisson de Faisans en Demi-Deuil, et
Cailles à la Trois Mousquetaires, Croustades avec Purées
d'Haricots Blancs et Rouges, Marrons et Petits Pois,
Sauces de Groseille,* Poivrade, et Essence de Truffes*

*Le Mélange Fameux de Pére Dumas**

Petits Fours Assortis en Paniers de Roses Sucres
Corbillons de Dattes, Noix, Oranges, et Raisins aux Chocolat
sur Nuage de Barbe à Papa
Boules de Glacé en Gaufrettes d'Escalope
Sorbets de Fruits en Fichu de Chocolat*

Café

Wines:

*Arrival Champagne: Taittinger Comtes de Champagne
With Soup: Dry Sack Sherry
With Salmon: Bonnes Mares Domaine Drouhin-Laroze, 1967
With Dessert: Château d'Yquem, 1966
After Dinner: Benedictine, Cognac, Pernod*

—

*The Lodge at Pebble Beach, Owners
Jean Louis Tourel, Chef de Cuisine*

The Cypress Room is in The Lodge at Pebble Beach, a resort justly famous for its many unique qualities: its beauty, its comfort, its great golfing facility, and its incomparable French cuisine. All of these are the result of the dedicated labor of a very talented group, prominent among whom is Jean Louis Tourel, the executive chef de cuisine at The Lodge.

Jean Louis has been with the Lodge since 1970 and is responsible for all menus in the elegant Cypress Room, the chic Club XIX, and for the many private dining events. A native of France, he served his apprenticeship at the Petite Auberge de Noves, a 3-Star Michelin restaurant in France at the time. In point of service and experience, Jean Louis is considered one of the 'deans of cuisine' on the Peninsula, and he looks the part.

The Cypress Room looks out across Monterey Bay to Point Lobos and the beginnings of the Santa Lucia Mountains. In this magnificent atmosphere it is appropriate that Jean Louis should select an opulent repast for the Cypress Room's contribution to this book. Every Christmas the restaurant stages the incredible Feast of Noel, devised in 1870 by Alexander Dumas Pere, the famous author of 'The Three Musketeers' and 'The Count of Monte Cristo' and internationally known bon vivant. He had delivered the menu and recipes to Anatole France in the spring of 1870 for publication, but died that December before 'Dumas Dictionaire de Cuisine' was published. Few restaurants in the world are capable of such an epicurean tour de force as Dumas' feast. It requires a large staff and an astounding array of exotic ingredients. It also requires reservations well in advance, at least three hours of eating time, and costs around $100 per person. The original menu consists of twenty-five courses in all, accompanied by at least seven wines; we have selected seven of the dishes and four wines from this array.

Joyeux Noel et Bon Appetit!

The Lodge at Pebble Beach
Pebble Beach

CREME DE TORTUE A L' EXTASE DU ROI POSEIDON,
GARNI DE CREVETTES, MOULES ET PALOURDES
(Cream of Turtle Soup, King Poseidon's Ecstasy, Garnished with
 Shrimp, Mussels and Clams)

2 pounds turtle meat, diced in 1/2 inch pieces
2-1/4 cups dry sherry
6 shallots, finely chopped
1 teaspoon finely chopped fresh sweet basil
1 cup plus 2 tablespoons sweet butter
8 mussels, shelled
8 clams, shelled
8 shrimp, shelled
1 bay leaf
4 cups chicken broth
3 tablespoons flour
4 egg yolks
1 cup heavy cream
1/2 teaspoon each, finely chopped: fresh rosemary, thyme,
    parsley, watercress
Few drops Tabasco—optional
Salt to taste

1. Marinate turtle meat in 2 cups sherry one hour.
2. Sauté chopped shallots and sweet basil in 6 tablespoons butter. Add
   mussels, clams and shrimp and cook, stirring, 5 minutes. Add 1/4 cup
   sherry, toss to blend and set aside.
3. In saucepan, melt 1/2 cup butter and glaze remaining shallots
   and bay leaf.
4. Add drained turtle meat, reserving marinade. Sauté 10 minutes.
5. Add chicken broth and cook 2 minutes longer.
6. Make a roux of 4 tablespoons butter and 3 tablespoons flour.
7. Beat egg yolks with heavy cream and combine with roux. Add dipper
   of soup to mixture, stir together, and return mixture to soup,
   blending well.
8. Add mussels, shrimp and clams. Add rosemary, thyme, parsley and
   watercress. Add marinade and Tabasco, if desired.
9. Salt to taste and blend well.

SAUMON A LA CHAMBORD DU CHATEAU MONTE CRISTO
AVEC CHAMPIGNONS TOURNES, PATE DE MARCASSIN,
QUENELLES DE SAUMON ET SAUCE GENEVOISE
(Whole Salmon, Braised in Red Wine, Served with Fluted Mushrooms,
Pâté of Wild Boar, Quenelles of Pink Salmon Mousse
and Sauce Genevoise)

6 tablespoons butter
1 tablespoon olive oil
2 onions, thinly sliced
2 stalks celery, thinly sliced
2 carrots, thinly sliced
2 small leeks, cut in thin strips
1 clove garlic, minced
2 whole cloves
2 whole allspice
1 6- to 7-pound salmon, cleaned, head and skin left on
Sprinkle of *Quatre Epices*
2 bay leaves
1 sprig fresh thyme, or 3/4 teaspoon dried
2 quarts red wine—enough to measure halfway up side of fish
    during cooking

1. Melt butter in bottom of large fish-cooker or shallow roasting pan.
   Add oil, vegetables, garlic, cloves and allspice and glaze over
   medium heat.
2. Sprinkle salmon with *Quatre Epices* and set in cooker "with its back
   towards the sun"—in an upright position—on top of vegetables.
3. Add bay leaves, thyme and wine. Bring to near boiling.
4. Remove from stove and cover fish with foil or wet parchment paper.
5. Place cooker in 350 degree oven and bake about 45 minutes or until
   salmon is done, basting every 6 minutes to insure a dark rich color.
6. Remove salmon and serve in traditional upright position on hot
   platter, with prescribed sauce and accompaniments.

QUATRE EPICES

1-1/2 ounces white pepper
1/4 teaspoon ground cloves
1/2 teaspoon ground ginger
3/4 teaspoon ground nutmeg

Combine all ingredients.

This recipe for "Four Spices" will make three ounces and will keep very well.

Fluted mushrooms are scored by hand, like pinwheels.

PATE DE MARCASSIN (Pâté of Wild Boar, or Piglet)

1 pound fresh young wild boar ham, or fresh young piglet ham
   —not over 5 months old
1/4 pound veal
3 shallots, chopped
1 small onion, chopped
1 clove garlic, minced
1 cup Cognac
1/4 cup Madeira
1 pound salt pork, half ground and half cut in strips
1/4 teaspoon dried thyme
1/4 teaspoon black pepper
1/4 teaspoon ground nutmeg
1/4 teaspoon fresh ginger, grated
1/4 teaspoon sage
2 eggs
1/4 teaspoon *Quatre Epices*
3 truffles
1/4 cup pistachio nuts, toasted
1 bay leaf
Toast rounds or toast points
Aspic Jelly

(continued on next page)

1. Dice young boar or piglet ham and veal into 1 inch pieces. Mix with combined shallots, onion, garlic, Cognac and Madeira, and marinate 3 hours.
2. Preheat oven to 350 degrees.
3. Drain meat from marinade and grind twice through finest blade of meat grinder or in food processor. Mix well with ground salt pork.
4. Strain marinade and reserve.
5. Place meats in a bowl. Add thyme, black pepper, nutmeg, ginger, sage, eggs and *Quatre Epices.* Chop 2 truffles and add. Add pistachios. Pour in marinade and mix well.
6. Line bottom of 2-quart casserole with strips of salt pork. Press pâté mixture on top. Cover with salt pork strips. Lay bay leaf over the top. Cover casserole; seal by tying 2 layers of foil around pan.
7. Place casserole, immersed in pan of hot water, in preheated oven. Bake for 1-1/2 hours, until pâté shrinks from sides of pan. Remove salt pork from the top and allow pâté to cool. Refrigerate for at least 24 hours.
8. To serve, scoop half-balls of pâté onto toast rounds, top with thin slices of truffle as garnish, and coat the whole with *Aspic Jelly.* Chill. Serve with *Braised Salmon.*

ASPIC JELLY

1 tablespoon plain gelatin
1/4 cup cold clear strong chicken broth
1 cup regular chicken broth
1/2 cup Madeira

1. Soak gelatin in extra-strength broth; stir to soften.
2. Heat regular-strength broth with wine. When hot, add to gelatin and stir until gelatin dissolves.
3. Chill in refrigerator until almost solid.
4. Brush rounds of pâté with mixture and refrigerate until aspic is completely set.

QUENELLES DE SAUMON

1 pound raw pink salmon, cleaned and boned
2 large egg whites, beaten
1-1/2 cups heavy cream
1 tablespoon salt
1/4 teaspoon freshly ground black pepper
2 drops Tabasco
Butter

1. Preheat oven to 350 degrees.
2. Grind salmon fine in food chopper or blender. Place in a bowl and beat thoroughly with wooden spoon. Set bowl in pan of finely cracked ice.
3. Stir in egg whites slowly, then heavy cream. Add salt, pepper and Tabasco.
4. Pour mixture into well-buttered shallow custard cups. Set cups in pan of hot water reaching half-way up sides of cups. Place in preheated oven and bake 45 minutes, or until knife inserted in mousse comes out clean.
5. Unmold and serve with *Braised Salmon.* Accompany with *Sauce Genevoise.*

SAUCE GENEVOISE

The secret of beautiful clear sauce is slow simmering.

2 cups *Fish Bouillon with Red Wine*
2 cups *Lenten Espagnole Sauce*
1/3 cup brandy
1 cup red wine
1 cup beef bouillon
1 tablespoon sweet butter
1 teaspoon anchovy paste

1. Mix *Fish Bouillon with Red Wine* with *Lenten Espagnole Sauce*,
   and simmer gently 1 hour. Strain through a colander, then through
   fine sieve to extract only the essence. Skim all fat from surface.
2. Carefully flame brandy. When extinguished, add wine and bouillon.
   Simmer slowly 1-1/2 hours, skimming off debris as it rises.
   Remove from heat and strain again, through very fine sieve or
   thin muslin cloth.
3. Finish with butter and anchovy paste. Blend well.

Tip: If this sauce becomes too heavy, it may be corrected with the
   addition of a little red wine.

FISH BOUILLON WITH RED WINE

3 small onions, chopped
4 carrots, peelings only
2 stalks celery, inner tender stalks only, chopped
1/2 stick butter
1 pound salmon heads, trimmings and other fishbones
1 quart good dry red wine

1. Combine onions, carrot peelings and celery. Sauté in butter until
   browned.
2. Add salmon heads, trimmings and other fishbones. Cover and cook
   slowly 20 minutes. Shake pan to prevent sticking.
3. Tip pan to drain off butter. Pour in wine. Simmer until liquid is
   reduced to 2 cups. Strain and reserve bouillon.
4. Use as directed in *Sauce Genevoise*.

LENTEN ESPAGNOLE SAUCE

1-1/2 cups finely chopped onions
1 cup finely chopped carrots
1/4 cup finely chopped parsley
1 teaspoon dried thyme
2 bay leaves
2 cloves garlic
1 whole allspice
1-1/2 sticks butter, melted
3/4 cup flour
2 cups white wine
3 tablespoons tomato paste
4 cups beef bouillon
1/2 teaspoon black pepper
Salt to taste
1 tablespoon sweet butter

1. Sauté vegetables with thyme, bay leaves, garlic and allspice in melted
   butter. When well-browned, add flour and stir over medium heat until
   roux begins to brown slightly, to the color of hazelnuts.
2. Add wine, tomato paste, bouillon and pepper. Stir thoroughly and
   bring to a boil. Lower heat and simmer for 1-1/2 hours. Salt to
   taste and strain through a fine sieve.
3. Add sweet butter and stir well. Lightly brush surface with a little
   additional butter to prevent skin from forming.
4. Use as directed in *Sauce Genevoise.*

To serve—

Heat platter. Set salmon upright and brush with hot *Genevoise Sauce*
to glaze. Surround with parsley and circle with Fluted Mushrooms,
Pate of Wild Boar, and Quenelles of Pink Salmon Mousse. Serve
with *Sauce Genevoise.*

LE MELANGE FAMEUX DU PERE DUMAS
(Pére Dumas' Famous Salad)

2 cooked beets, sliced thin
1/2 cup celery, sliced into half-moons
1/4 cup minced truffles
1/2 cup grated celery root
2 small boiled potatoes, peeled and sliced thin
1 bunch Bibb lettuce
Pinch paprika
Dumas' Secret Dressing

Toss salad lightly. Sprinkle with paprika and dress with *Dumas Secret Dressing.*

DUMAS SECRET DRESSING

2 eggs, hard-boiled
1/2 cup olive oil
2 teaspoons chopped chervil
1/4 cup canned flaked tuna, crushed
3 anchovy filets, mashed
2 teaspoons Maille mustard
1 tablespoon soy sauce
2 tablespoons finely chopped small gherkins
1/4 cup finest vinegar available
Pepper to taste

1. In an empty salad bowl, mash egg yolks with oil to form paste. Add chervil, tuna, anchovies, mustard, soy, gherkins and chopped egg whites.
2. Thin with vinegar. Add pepper to taste.

Tip: Maille mustard is comparable to Dijon; for vinegar, we believe the finest available is white rice vinegar.

There you have my salad of such great imagination, which so fascinates my friends," were the words Alexandre Dumas left with his "Secret Recipe."

PETITS FOURS

Traditionally *Petits Fours* are decorated with chocolate rosettes and candied violets. Their aura of elegant celebration justifies the elaborate preparation.

GATEAU MOSCOVITE (Sponge Cake)

1 cup plus 1 tablespoon cake flour
1/2 teaspoon salt
1-3/4 sticks cold sweet butter
Peel of 1 lemon, finely grated
6 eggs, separated
1/2 cup plus 2 tablespoons sugar
1/2 teaspoon vanilla extract
1/2 teaspoon cream of tartar
2 cups apricot jam
4 teaspoons lemon juice
1 cup fresh raspberry jam
2 tablespoons apricot liqueur
1/4 cup Cointreau
Chocolate Butter Cream
2 tablespoons raspberry liqueur
8 ounces *Almond Paste*—or commercial almond paste or marzipan
Powdered sugar
8 ounces *Kirsch Butter Cream*

1. Preheat oven to 350 degrees.
2. Butter and flour 2 9-inch square cake pans, or an 8 x 11-inch oblong.
3. Sift cake flour and 1/2 teaspoon salt onto waxed paper on breadboard.
4. Cut 1-3/4 sticks butter into thin strips, then dice across smaller, and again smaller. Cut into flour and salt until you have a fine blend. Be sure butter remains cold. At no time should butter and flour become a paste. Refrigerate until ready to use.
5. Add lemon peel to egg yolks. Add scant 1/4 cup sugar and beat until all the sugar has disappeared. Yolks should be very, very stiff. Add vanilla, and blend.

(continued on next page)

6. Beat egg whites at room temperature with a pinch of salt. After 1 minute, add cream of tartar. Continue beating at medium speed 3 minutes more. Turn beater to high speed and slowly add another scant 1/4 cup sugar. Beat until whites form firm peaks. Stop beater.
7. Put flour/butter mixture on top of egg whites. Top with beaten egg yolks and fold together lightly.
8. Divide batter between pans, smooth the surface and bake 30 minutes. Turn out on racks to cool.
9. Meanwhile: *for the first cake,* boil apricot jam with 1 tablespoon sugar. Stir in 2 teaspoons lemon juice. *For second cake,* boil raspberry jam with 1 tablespoon sugar, then stir in remaining 2 teaspoons lemon juice.
10. *To assemble first cake*, slice cooled layer in half, sprinkle with apricot liqueur, and spread boiling apricot jam over bottom half. Now set other half on top and press gently. Sprinkle with 2 tablespoons Cointreau. Cut into 1-inch squares and ice with *Chocolate Butter Cream.*

    To assemble second cake, slice remaining layer in half. Sprinkle bottom half with raspberry liqueur and spread with boiling raspberry jam. Set remaining half-layer on top and press gently. Now sprinkle with 2 tablespoons Cointreau. Roll out *Almond Paste* very thin on a baking sheet sprinkled with powdered sugar. Turn onto top of cake and trim edges. Cut into 1-inch squares. Ice with *Kirsch Butter Cream.*
11. Store cakes in refrigerator until ready to serve.

CHOCOLATE BUTTER CREAM

3 ounces bittersweet chocolate, grated
1/4 cup water
1/3 cup sugar
4 egg yolks
2 sticks sweet butter, softened

1. Melt chocolate in bowl over pan of hot water. Stir until melted. Set to one side.
2. Bring water and sugar to quick boil and cook 2 minutes.
3. Beat egg yolks. Slowly pour sugar syrup over yolks, beating at medium speed. Turn beater to high speed and continue beating 6 minutes more, until mixture is thick and pale yellow.
4. Add butter a little at a time, at low speed. Increase to medium speed and beat until smooth.
5. Keep cream in a cool place until ready to use.

ALMOND PASTE

1/2 pound blanched almonds, ground
3 bitter almonds, ground
1 pound powdered sugar
1-1/2 teaspoons Marasquin
1-1/2 teaspoons Orange Water

1. Combine almonds and bitter almonds with sugar. Grind twice, the first time through large-holed blade of grinder, the second time using the next smaller-sized blade.
2. Place on breadboard and knead in half of powdered sugar at a time. Add Marasquin and Orange Water.
3. Grind a third and fourth time through finest blade of grinder. Cover with a damp cloth and set in refrigerator until ready to use.

KIRSCH BUTTER CREAM

1/4 cup water
1/2 cup sugar
4 egg yolks
2 sticks sweet butter, softened
3 tablespoons Kirsch

1. Bring water and sugar to quick boil. Boil 2 minutes.
2. Beat egg yolks. Slowly, pour sugar syrup over yolks, beating at medium speed. Turn to high speed and beat 8 minutes more, until mixture is thick and pale yellow.
3. With beaters at low speed, add butter a little at a time. Increase to medium speed and beat until smooth. Add Kirsch.
4. Keep cream in a cool place until ready to use.

DEETJEN'S
BIG SUR INN

Dinner for Six

Cream of Celery Soup

Red Lettuce Salad
with
Imported Danish Blue Cheese

Lamb Stew

Red Cabbage

Strawberry Freeze with Fresh Mint

Wine:

Stag's Leap Wine Cellars Merlot, 1975

Ed and Kuniyo Gardien, Innkeepers
Bill de Groat, Cook

There are places that may be more 'in' or elegant, but nowhere else is there a place like Deetjen's Big Sur Inn. It's a retreat from the troubles of the world where one can rest and feed body and soul.

Even when fog hides the creek or catches in the tops of the giant redwoods, it is warm beside the fire in the Inn's rustic dining rooms. Meals are served on Royal Staffordshire china, while soft classical music completes the atmosphere of good taste and friendliness.

Built in the early 1930's by the Deetjen's, Big Sur Inn sits beside Castro Creek, roughly thirty miles south of Carmel on scenic Highway 1. While that highway was being carved out of the cliffs overlooking the Pacific, Helen and Helmuth Deetjen fed many of the hungry highway workers. Later, the Inn housed the great and not-so-great from around the world. The Deetjen's intuitive hospitality is continued today by innkeepers Ed and Kuniyo Gardien and by Bill DeGroat, the cook. All three knew and worked with 'Grandpa' Deetjen during the last years of his life.

Both Ed and Bill came to the Inn in 1964. Bill says humbly, "They needed a cook, so I began cooking." Even the Modigliani hanging in the kitchen gives no hint of Bill's talents as sculptor, a student of history, physical anthropology, and Japanese. His cooking, nevertheless, takes a back seat to none.

To dine at Big Sur Inn is to feel the very essence of the Big Sur, as espoused by a local poet and captured in the plaque on the Inn's wall that reads:

> It is not so much that men should pass through here but once,
> To rest their bones and fill their bellies
> But more to remember what was felt within,
> A place, a time, a memory, and over all of that
> A place to where one returns,
> Returns again for lack of finding anywhere else that is
> Quite the same.

Highway 1,
Big Sur

CREAM OF CELERY SOUP

1/2 pound butter
4 tablespoons flour
6 stalks celery, finely chopped
1-1/2 quarts milk
Salt and pepper

1. Saute′ celery until limp.
2. In a separate saucepan, make roux of butter and flour. Blend
   in milk and stir until smooth.
3. Add celery to creamy mixture and simmer over low heat.
4. Season with salt and pepper and serve.

RED LETTUCE SALAD WITH
IMPORTED DANISH BLUE CHEESE

2 heads red lettuce, washed and dried
2 sliced tomatoes
1/4 cup minced green onions
1/4 cup minced celery
1 cup minced red cabbage
Vinaigrette Dressing
Imported Danish blue cheese

1. Tear lettuce into bite-size pieces. Chill for at least an hour.
2. Lightly toss lettuce, tomatoes, green onions, celery and red cabbage.
3. Add chilled *Vinaigrette Dressing* and toss.
4. Grate blue cheese over the top for garnish.

DRESSING

1 cup salad oil
1/3 cup vinegar
3 cloves garlic, crushed
Salt, pepper, thyme, oregano

1. Mix all ingredients together and blend well.
2. Chill until ready to use.

***Don't use too much blue cheese or the salad will taste
too strong.***

LAMB STEW

3 tablespoons oil
4 pounds lamb stew meat
Flour to dredge
Salt, pepper, thyme, paprika, dill weed
3 tablespoons white wine
2 quarts lamb stock, cooked from bones
2 green peppers, chopped into 1-inch chunks
2 onions, cut into quarters
1 carrot, sliced
1 bunch parsley, chopped

1. Heat oil in saucepan.
2. Flour meat and brown in oil.
3. Season with salt, pepper, thyme, paprika and dill weed to taste.
4. Add wine and lamb stock and bring to a simmer.
5. Add peppers, onions, carrot and parsley. Continue simmering
   for 2 1/2 hours.

***In California, where rapid change is the rule, people appreciate a
place where traditions are kept. Often people who came to the Inn on
their honeymoon ten or twenty years before are pleasantly surprised to
enjoy the same menu and music that they discovered originally.***

RED CABBAGE

4 pounds red cabbage
Salt and pepper
1 quart apple cider vinegar
2 onions, chopped
2 green apples, chopped
1/2 slice bacon
4 tablespoons brown sugar

1. Shred cabbage; add salt and pepper. Add vinegar and bring to
   a boil.
2. Add remaining ingredients and cook for 1 hour over medium heat.
3. Remove from heat and cool for 2 to 3 hours.
4. Refrigerate in glass container overnight.
5. Warm and serve.

***This is better the second or third day. We always make enough
to last.***

STRAWBERRY FREEZE WITH FRESH MINT

1 quart Knudsen's Strawberry Freeze or Ice
Four sprigs fresh mint

FOX HILL

Dinner for Eight

Quenelles of Sole

Artichoke Soup

*House Salad
with
Green Goddess Dressing*

Chateaubriand President

Champignon Provençale

Pommes Dauphine

Toro de Oro

Flaming Fox Tail

Wines:
With Appetizer: Coron Pére et Fils Saint Veran
With Entrée: Henri Delnaud Château Ferrande, 1971 or 1973

David Macmillan and Gerard Guijarro, Owners
Chester Gillette, Maître d'
Gerard Guijarro, Chef

This low rambling California-style inn eight miles east of Carmel has drawn customers since it was built in 1946, but never to the degree that it does today. The charming Fox Hill Restaurant is one of the main reasons, and the two energetic young owners—David MacMillan and Gerard Guijarro—is the other. Acquiring the inn in 1978, they created a gourmet restaurant, recruiting their families as workers, and brought the entire inn to life as an outstanding country resort for relaxing in the sun, tennis, swimming, hot-tubbing . . . and just fine eating.

A native Californian, David MacMillan first studied to be a lawyer, but was side-tracked when he became intrigued by the restaurant business. He has learned the operation from every aspect, from busboy to maitre d' and, ultimately, management.

Gerard Guijarro's career has been adventuresome. He grew up and was apprenticed in what he calls 'the French gastronomique capital'—Lyon, France. While in Tahiti serving in the French Foreign Legion, he mastered both Polynesian and Chinese cuisine as a sideline. When his tour of duty was over, Gerard stayed in Tahiti, working at l'Auberge de la Punaruu, Club Med, and La Pizzeria. He opened an all-night bistro called the Champagne Club, was proprietor of Les Ramparts for a time and, before leaving Tahiti, served as chef on several elegant chartered South Seas sailing vessels. He came to La Mirabelle in San Francisco in 1972, and to Carmel in 1974 as chef at the Covey.

David and Gerard's philosophy that "cooking is an art, and all art is patience," makes Fox Hill a great addition to the Monterey Peninsula restaurants for resident and tourist alike.

Carmel Valley Road at Los Laureles Grade
Carmel

QUENELLES OF SOLE

1 pound filet of fresh sole
1 recipe of *Panade*, prepared ahead and refrigerated at least
   24 hours before use
5 egg whites, beaten
1/2 cup heavy cream
Salt and cayenne to taste
Flour
Salted water
Sauce Normande, warmed

1. Shred or blend sole until smooth.
2. Add *Panade*, little by little, alternating with beaten egg whites
   and then heavy cream until all is used. Add salt and cayenne
   and beat until very smooth and thick, adding more egg whites
   if mixture becomes too thick.
3. Lightly flour breadboard. Shape fish mixture into soupspoon-
   sized dumplings—approximately 1-1/2 x 3 inches—and roll in
   flour, shaking off any excess.
4. Boil water in large saucepan, add salt, lower heat and poach
   dumplings for 8 to 12 minutes, or until cooked through. Be sure
   not to boil, or the dumplings will fall apart.
5. Serve with *Sauce Normande.*

PANADE

1 quart milk
2/3 cup butter
2-3/4 cups flour
8 eggs, whole

1. Combine milk and butter. Bring to a boil, melting all of the butter.
   Remove and add flour all at once. Stir hard, until mixture forms
   into a ball.
2. Return to stove; keep stirring hard, until all dough loosens from
   side of pot, and dough sticks together. Remove and cool for
   5 minutes.
3. Add eggs one at a time, stirring after each addition until the
   egg disappears.
4. Refrigerate until ready to use, at least 24 hours.

SAUCE NORMANDE

1 cup sliced fresh mushrooms
1 fresh shallot, finely chopped
2 tablespoons plus 1 tablespoon butter
1/4 cup brandy
1 tablespoon flour
1/2 cup heavy cream
1/4 cup baby shrimp
1/4 teaspoon salt
1/8 teaspoon white pepper

1. In small saucepan, cook mushrooms and shallots in 2 tablespoons butter for 2 minutes. Remove pan from fire.
2. Add brandy and flame.
3. Mix flour with remaining butter to form a roux. Add heavy cream and cook at least 5 minutes, until mixture thickens. Add mushrooms, shallots and shrimp. Season and serve warm with *Quenelles of Sole*, as directed.

You might like this recipe with Crayfish Sauce Nantua, which can be purchased at gourmet shops.

ARTICHOKE SOUP

1/4 pound butter
3 medium white onions, diced
2 leeks, using all of white and 3/4 of green, diced
5 medium artichokes, leaves only
4 potatoes, diced
Water to cook
Salt and white pepper
Juice from 2 lemons
2 bay leaves
1/2 cup whipping cream

1. Melt butter in soup pot. Sauté diced onions and leeks in butter until steamed. Add artichoke leaves and potatoes. Cover with water and add salt and pepper, lemon juice and bay leaves. Bring to a boil; lower heat and simmer 1-1/2 to 2 hours.
2. Drain, separating liquid from vegetables and reserving both.
3. Blend vegetables in blender and return to liquid. Cook an additional 30 minutes, until flesh of artichoke leaves separates from the leaf fibre. Strain through a sieve and discard fibre.
4. Finish with cream. Blend well. If more thickening is desired, make a roux and add, or use *Beurre Manié.*
5. Adjust seasoning if necessary, and serve hot.

BEURRE MANIE

Mix together equal amounts of flour and butter. Form into small egg shapes. Keep refrigerated. Flour will not lump when added in this fashion. These little 'eggs' of butter and flour may be used in place of a roux to thicken soups and sauces.

HOUSE SALAD WITH GREEN GODDESS DRESSING

Select greens, wash, dry, crisp, and toss together.

GREEN GODDESS DRESSING

1 filet of anchovy, chopped
6 green onions, finely chopped
Juice of 2 lemons—more or less, to taste
1 cup sour cream
1 cup mayonnaise
2 soupspoons cider vinegar
Dash white pepper
Dash salt
Dash Accent—optional
Fresh parsley, finely chopped—optional

1. Combine anchovy and onions. Add lemon juice. Combine with remaining ingredients and mix well.
2. Add parsley if you desire greener appearance.

This is a delicate dressing.

CHATEAUBRIAND PRESIDENT

Basic puff pastry recipe for 4, prepared ahead or purchased frozen
4 large fresh shallots, diced
8 cloves garlic, finely diced
1/4 cup finely chopped fresh parsley
1/2 cup olive oil
1-1/3 cups crabmeat
8 large fresh tomatoes, diced
20 mushrooms, sliced
Cayenne pepper to taste
Salt to taste
12 large soupspoons white wine
4 large soupspoons brandy
Breadcrumbs, as desired
Butter
4 2-pound filets of beef
Salt and white pepper
Garnish: watercress

1. Keep puff pastry refrigerated until ready to use.
2. *Prepare stuffing:* Glaze shallots, then garlic, then parsley in olive oil. Stir to prevent scorching. Add crabmeat and cook about 3 minutes. Add diced tomatoes and mushrooms, stirring with each addition. Season with cayenne and salt, and remove from heat. Add wine and 3 soupspoons of brandy, and flame. Return to heat and cook at a slow boil 10 minutes. Add breadcrumbs—at your discretion—to form stuffing. Cool and reserve.
3. Preheat oven to 500 degrees.
4. Melt butter in hot sauté pan and brown beef filets, one at a time, on both sides. Season with salt and white pepper to taste.
5. Place in preheated oven and cook to desired doneness—10 minutes for rare, 12 to 15 minutes for medium rare, or 20 minutes for well-done. Turn every 5 minutes to cook evenly. Remove and drain away grease. Flame with remaining brandy.
6. Roll out puff pastry to 3/8 inch thickness. Place on greased pastry sheets. Each pastry should measure 6 to 7 inches by 12 inches.
7. Cut a slit lengthwise in each filet, about halfway through the thickness of the meat. Fill with stuffing. Center a filet on each pastry oblong.

8. Fold pastry filet, joining edges. Pinch ends to seal.
9. Bake in 450 degree oven 10 to 15 minutes, or until browned.
10. To serve, slice crosswise, and garnish with watercress.

Tip: Durkee makes a puff dough which can be found in the frozen
food section of most grocery stores.

***Electric ovens tend to burn pastry, so top filets with aluminum
foil at beginning of baking period, removing for the last few minutes
for pastry to turn a golden brown.***

CHAMPIGNON PROVENCALE

1 pound fresh mushrooms, sliced
2 tablespoons butter
2 large shallots
2 or more cloves garlic, chopped
1 tablespoon brandy
1 large soupspoon white wine
Salt and white pepper to taste

1. Sauté mushrooms in butter; add shallots and garlic. Cook 2 to 3
   minutes, stirring constantly.
2. Remove pan from stove. Pour in brandy and wine, and flame.
3. Season with salt and white pepper to taste, and serve.

***White pepper is used for vegetables and sauces because it has a finer
consistency than black pepper, but care must be taken not to forget
that you have added it since it blends into the color of the food!***

POMME DAUPHINE

1 recipe *Pâte Choux*
4 russet potatoes, peeled
Cold water
Salt
Pinch of nutmeg
4 egg yolks
1 beaten egg white
French breadcrumbs, salted to taste
Oil for deep frying

1. Prepare *Pâte Choux.*
2. Boil potatoes, starting in cold salted water.
3. Preheat oven to 400 degrees.
4. When potatoes are cooked but not mushy, remove and drain.
5. Crush potatoes in the pan, and bake in preheated oven for 5 minutes to remove moisture.
6. Place potatoes in large pot, add nutmeg and egg yolks, and beat well. Combine with *Pâte Choux* until well-blended. Cool.
7. Shape potato mixture into small rolls the size of a soupspoon, or into small croquettes. Dip in beaten egg white, then salted breadcrumbs. Refrigerate until ready to fry.
8. Deep fry, and drain. Serve hot.

PATE CHOUX

1 pint water
1/4 cup butter
Pinch of salt and white pepper
2-1/4 cups flour
6 or 7 whole eggs, at room temperature

1. Combine water, butter, salt and white pepper in heavy saucepan. Bring to a boil.
2. Remove from heat and pour in flour all at once. Mix well with wooden spoon.
3. Return to low heat and beat rapidly and vigorously while cooking. Mixture will lose rough look and become smooth. When it becomes dry and leaves sides of the pan, remove from heat again. *Do not overcook* or dough may fail to puff up.
4. Add eggs one at a time, beating briskly after each addition until slippery look disappears.
5. Use in preparation of potatoes as directed.

TORO DE ORO

8 egg whites
Pinch of salt
1/4 cup plus 4 teaspoons powdered sugar
2 egg yolks
Vanilla extract
24 ladyfingers
8 scoops ice cream
1 ounce each: Curacao, rum, and brandy

1. Preheat oven to 500 degrees.
2. For each egg white, add a small pinch of salt and beat until stiff.
   Gradually add 1/4 cup powdered sugar and whip hard.
3. In separate bowl, whip egg yolks with remaining powdered sugar,
   add vanilla to taste, and continue beating with a fork until
   thickened.
4. *Very* lightly, fold the two mixtures together.
5. Arrange 3 ladyfingers per serving on ovenproof plates. Top each
   with a scoop of ice cream. *Quickly*—speed is important—shape
   egg mixture into a 'mountain' over ice cream, being sure to
   cover completely.
6. Pop immediately into preheated oven, and bake until 'mountain'
   peaks become golden brown. Remove at once. Pour slightly
   warmed liquors—which have been flamed—over 'mountains'
   and serve.

FLAMING FOX TAIL

Per drink—

Lime juice
Sugar
1/2 ounce Bacardi 151 proof rum
1 ounce Tia Maria
Strong coffee

1. Dip glass rims in lime juice, then into sugar.
2. Add rum and Tia Maria, tip glass and flame for 10 seconds.
3. Fill to the top with strong coffee and serve.

Dinner for Six

Mushrooms à la Crème George

Potage Cultivateur

Tossed Salad Greens
with
French Dressing

Coq au Vin
with
Boiled Potatoes

Crêpes Suzette

Wine:

With Entrée: Robert Mondavi Pinot Noir

Paul Johnson, Owner/Manager
James Thorsen, Chef

If there is one restaurant on the Peninsula that can be called 'historic,' it has to be Gallatin's in the old Stokes Adobe, located in the heart of Monterey—"half-way between the hospital and the jail." The adobe was built in the 1830's by an Englishman, Dr. James Stokes, and bought years later by the Escolles family. Then, at the turn of the century, the Sargent Gragg family acquired it and lived there for many years.

After World War II, Gallatin Powers leased the lovely old adobe and Gallatin's Restaurant was born. It is still one of the few places in America where such epicurian delights as Whole Suckling Pig, Imperial Wild Boar and Bull's Head Minotaur can be enjoyed, with a twenty-four hour notice. Stepping into the dining rooms or into the bar is stepping back into old Monterey. The famous and infamous of Monterey are represented in the names of Gallatin's specialties—Joaquin Murieta's Dinner, Hypolite Bouchard's Dinner, Thomas O. Larkin's Dinner, and more.

The decor, the service—the total ambiance—reflect the tradition of Montereño hospitality. And for those so inclined, there is often a sing-along around the piano in Gallatin's Bar.

Mr. Paul Johnson is the owner and manager of Gallatin's now, and chef James Thorsen—a graduate of the Cordon Bleu School in Paris—joins him in presenting a memorable dining experience.

500 Hartnell Avenue
Monterey

MUSHROOMS A LA CREME GEORGE

1/2 pound whole small mushrooms
Butter
1 teaspoon sherry
1/2 cup sour cream
Salt and pepper to taste
Heart-shaped croutons for garnish

1. Saute' mushrooms in butter.
2. Pour off grease and add sherry. Cook 1 minute, add sour cream
   and reduce all the liquid to a sauce consistency.
3. Season to taste and serve with heart shaped croutons.

POTAGE CULTIVATEUR

3 leeks
2 carrots
1/2 head cabbage
1 turnip
1 stalk celery
1/4 pound butter
Water
1/4 pound slab bacon
1 cup fresh green beans
2 potatoes
Salt to taste
Chervil leaves
Croutons
Grated Swiss cheese

1. Dice all the vegetables.
2. Sauté leeks, carrots, cabbage, turnip and celery in butter until soft but not browned. Add water to cover vegetables by 1 inch. Add bacon slab and cook for 1 hour.
3. When done, remove bacon and dice, removing any cartilage if necessary.
4. Return bacon to the pot, add beans and potatoes and cook 15 to 20 minutes longer.
5. Season with salt.
6. Serve topped with chervil leaves. Accompany with croutons and cheese, served separately.

You may substitute peas for the green beans.

TOSSED SALAD GREENS
WITH FRENCH DRESSING

Greens of your choice

Select, wash, dry and chill lettuce greens. When ready to serve, toss with *French Dressing.*

FRENCH DRESSING

1 cup oil
1/3 cup vinegar
1/2 teaspoon pepper
1 teaspoon dry mustard
Juice of 1/2 lemon
Salt

1. Mix all ingredients except salt.
2. Add salt to taste after other ingredients are well blended.

COQ AU VIN

2 chickens, sectioned
Marinade
1/4 cup salad oil
1/2 pound slab bacon, diced
Flour
1/4 pound small whole mushrooms
1/4 pound small whole white pearl onions, peeled
Garnish: fresh parsley, finely chopped

1. Marinate the chicken sections overnight, covering the mixture with oil so the wine has no contact with the air.
2. The next day, drain off the *Marinade,* separating chicken and vegetables from marinade liquid. Reserve separately.
3. Sauté diced bacon until browned and set aside, reserving the grease.
4. Blend enough flour into bacon grease to form a roux. Cook carefully until browned.
5. In a large saucepan, blend the marinade liquid with the roux. Bring to a boil, then lower heat to simmer.
6. Add vegetables and chicken and cook slowly until the chicken is done, approximately 30 to 45 minutes.
7. While the chicken is cooking, sauté mushrooms and set aside with cooked bacon. Boil onions, glaze in butter and set aside with mushrooms and bacon.

(continued on next page)

8. When chicken is done, remove from the sauce and set aside with mushrooms, onions and bacon. Cover to keep warm.
9. Continue cooking the sauce, removing all grease as it rises to the surface; this is time consuming, but must be done completely.
10. Season to taste with salt and pepper and filter through a sieve so that the sauce is velvety smooth.
11. When ready to serve, arrange chicken, mushrooms, onions and bacon on serving plate, cover with sauce and garnish with a sprinkle of fresh parsley.
12. Serve with boiled potatoes, cut in the shape of small footballs.

WINE MARINADE

2 onions, sliced
2 carrots, sliced
4 cloves garlic, crushed
Bouquet garni of parsley, celery, thyme and bay leaf
1 teaspoon cracked black pepper
1-1/2 bottles Burgundy

As with most red wine sauces, Coq au Vin sauce benefits from reheating. We reheat our sauce three times before we serve it. If you need to thin the sauce, be sure to use chicken stock and not wine.

We cut the potatoes by hand but you may want to substitute small boiled new potatoes.

CREPES SUZETTE

Crêpes should be prepared in advance.

1 cup flour
3 eggs
1–1/2 cups milk
2 ounces butter, melted and cooled
Pinch baking powder—optional
Sugar to taste
Butter

1. Mix flour and milk to the smooth consistency of cream.
2. Add eggs and sugar and blend well. Filter if necessary.
3. Add the melted and cooled butter. Let stand for 30 minutes. Thin with more milk only if necessary.
4. Coat a hot, buttered crêpe pan with batter and cook over a medium-high heat until edge of crêpe begins to release. Flip, and cook on the other side. Remove from pan and hold until ready to prepare *Sauce.*

SAUCE

Prepare the *Sauce* at tableside for a dramatic effect.

2 teaspoons sugar
4 ounces butter
1 orange, grated peel and juice
1 lemon, grated peel and juice
1 ounce Curacao
1 ounce Cointreau
1 ounce Kirschwasser
Powdered sugar

1. Melt butter in pre-heated pan. Add sugar, grated orange and lemon peels. Add orange and lemon juices. Blend.
2. Mix liqueurs together and add one-half of the mixture to the pan. Just before it reaches a boil, remove from flame. Ignite the alcohol after the pan has cooled slightly and let the flame burn away the alcohol completely.
3. Fold crêpes in quarters and add to pan.
4. Pour second half of the liqueur mixture into pan and repeat the flaming process.
5. Serve crêpes on dessert plates, dust with powdered sugar and cover with warm sauce from pan.

Alcohol should be ignited only after the pan has been removed from the open flame and allowed to cool down a bit. To ignite, bring the lighted match up from beneath the pan, close to the rim. The alcohol will "catch" just as the flame reaches the rim lip. We use a long handled crepe pan and keep it at a safe distance from our guests.

L'Escargot

Dinner for Four

Moules Marinière

Soupe de Tomates

Salade d'Endives

Poulet à la Crème avec Truffles

Ratatouille Provençale

Mousse au Chocolat

Wines:

With Appetizer, Soup and Salad: Muscadet
With Entrée: Gewurztraminer or Beaujolais

Yvan Nopert and André Francot, Owners, Maître d's and Chefs

A famous restaurant critic described L'Escargot as "perhaps the most accurate replica of a true French country restaurant in all California." This aptly describes the charmingly decorated and intimately proportioned dining rooms of L'Escargot on Mission Street in Carmel; the search to locate it is part of its charm, and well worth the trouble.

Yvan Nopert and André Francot are co-owners, co-maîtres d', and co-chefs—in fact, co-everything that makes this little restaurant wonderful. M. Nopert received his early culinary training in his native Belgium and served as chef in the Belgian Embassy in Washington, D.C. before opening L'Escargot in 1958. M. Francot, who is French, received his training both in Belgium and France, then made his way to Carmel via Montreal and has been co-owner of L'Escargot since 1969.

Yvan and André have become justly famous for their deliciously simple and honestly French cuisine. They personally supervise everything that is served to their customers, and insist on careful selection of produce, meats, poultry, fish and vegetables. Their "in-house" desserts are the crowning glory of their meals.

Mission Street, near Fourth
Carmel

MOULES MARINIERE

1/2 bunch celery, chopped
1 large onion, chopped
1/4 pound butter
8 pounds mussels in their shells
1/2 cup water
1 cup dry white wine
2 teaspoons ground pepper
5 soupspoons chopped parsley

1. In a large casserole, sauté celery and onion in butter until translucent but not brown.
2. Add mussels, water, wine and pepper. Cover and cook on high heat about 10 minutes or until all mussels are open. Stir every 2 or 3 minutes while cooking to mix mussels.
3. Add parsley and serve.

SOUPE DE TOMATES

1/2 bunch celery, chopped
2 large onions, chopped
Oil
4 pounds tomatoes, chopped
4 cloves garlic
2 teaspoons thyme
4 bay leaves
1 large potato, peeled and chopped

1. Sauté celery and onion in small amount of oil until translucent.
2. Add tomatoes, garlic, thyme, bay leaves and potato. Cover with water and salt and pepper to taste. Bring to a boil, lower heat and cook for 1 1/2 hours.
3. Strain through a coarse sieve and check seasoning.

SALADE d'ENDIVE WITH VINAIGRETTE DRESSING

4 Belgian endive
Olive oil
Wine vinegar
Salt and pepper

1. Wash and dry endive. Slice lengthwise and toss lightly with
   a vinaigrette dressing made of oil, vinegar, salt and pepper.
2. Arrange on individual salad plates and serve.

POULET A LA CREME AVEC TRUFFLES

2 2-pound fryers
2 pounds mushrooms, cut into large pieces
2 tablespoons butter
1 pint heavy cream
2 ounces Madeira
4 teaspoons chopped truffle peelings
Salt and pepper

1. Roast chickens in oven at 375 degrees until done. Drain away grease
   and cut into nice leg-and-breast serving portions.
2. Sauté mushroom pieces in butter and drain well.
3. Place chicken, Madeira, truffles, drained mushrooms and about
   90% of the cream into frying pan. Cook over high heat until cream
   thickens to a sauce consistency, stirring occasionally.
4. Remove chicken to serving dish. Salt and pepper sauce to taste.
   If sauce appears too thick, add remainder of cream, give it a last
   boil and pour over chicken and serve.

***It is important to avoid any of the grease from the chicken or
butter from the mushrooms when making the sauce, so drain well.

RATATOUILLE PROVENCAL

The vegetables in *Ratatouille* should be stewed and not fried. When cooking has been completed, most of the oil should have been absorbed.

2 large onions, sliced
1 eggplant, cut into bite-size pieces
1 yellow squash, sliced
3 tomatoes, peeled and quartered
2 red or green pimentos, sliced
Olive oil
Salt and pepper

1. Sauté onions in plenty of oil in frying pan, making sure oil is not too hot. When onions become soft, add pimentos and eggplant and simmer for 10 minutes.
2. Add tomatoes, cover, and simmer for 30 minutes. Remove cover and cook for an additional 10 minutes.

MOUSSE AU CHOCOLAT

6 ounces (6 squares) semi-sweet chocolate
2 tablespoons water
4 large eggs, separated
3/4 cup heavy cream
Sugar to taste

1. Combine the chocolate and water in top of a double boiler. Place over hot water and stir until chocolate is melted.
2. Beat egg yolks until light, then gradually beat into melted chocolate. Remove from heat.
3. Beat egg whites until stiff, then fold into the chocolate mixture.
4. Whip 1/2 cup cream and fold in. Add sugar to taste.
5. Spoon the *Mousse* into sherbet glasses and chill until ready to serve. Garnish with the remaining 1/4 cup of heavy cream, whipped and sweetened to taste.

Maison BERGERAC

Dinner for Four

Crème d'Oseille

Matelote de Poisson Regional

Daube Camarguise

Courgettes au Vert

(Salade)

(Assorted Cheeses)

Profiteroles au Chocolat

(Cafe Noir)

Wine:

With Soup & Fish: Boeckel-Alsace Pinot Gris
With Daube: Clos Vougeot
With Dessert: Taittinger Champagne, Brut

Raymond Bergerac, Owner and Chef de Cuisine

In 1892, Dr. Andrew J. Hart built one of the finest and most ornate three-story Victorian homes in California. In 1970, Raymond and Betty Bergerac, vacationing on the Peninsula with their four children, fell in love with the old Hart home, found it was for sale, and bought it. And Maison Bergerac was born.

Today, Chef Raymond, hostess Betty and waiters Daniel, Suzanne, Lucie and Janine Bergerac operate one of the most unique and delightful restaurants to be found anywhere. On weekend evenings, twenty-four fortunate diners assemble at Maison Bergerac for a feast at tables reserved for them alone for the entire evening. Reservations must be made months in advance because of the heavy demand. Dinner is a fixed price for everything, including appropriate aperitifs and wines to complement the evening's meal. Chef Bergerac attends to the selection of each outstanding menu, and the young Bergeracs serve with warm hospitality amid the romantic and colorful furnishings that make this Victorian home so special. Betty Bergerac welcomes guests with gracious warmth while keeping a practiced eye on all of the beautifully appointed tables.

Chef Raymond Bergerac's culinary career began in his native Alsace and took him to such notable restaurants as the Palais Hotel in Biarritz, The Clavel in Bordeaux, The Nassau Hotel on Long Island, and The Ambassador Hotel in Los Angeles. His talents have been recognized by membership in the Chaine des Rotisseurs and the Order Mondial des Gourmets Propagandistes des Vins.

Dining at Maison Bergerac is dining in style.

Lighthouse at 19th
Pacific Grove

CREME D' OSEILLE
(Fresh Sorrel Soup)

2 cups chopped fresh sorrel
2 potatoes, peeled and diced
2 leeks, chopped—use white parts only
2 tablespoons butter
6 cups poultry stock
1/2 cup dry vermouth
1 cup heavy cream
Salt and pepper to taste

Garnish: 1 tablespoon minced fresh sorrel

1. Sauté sorrel, potatoes and leeks in butter.
2. Add poultry stock and simmer 20 minutes.
3. Put through a food mill. Add vermouth, cream and salt and
   pepper to taste.
4. Heat and serve, garnished with minced sorrel.

***Sorrel grows beautifully in sandy soil in Maison Bergerac's garden,
and we use it in various dishes.***

MATELOTE DE POISSON REGIONAL
(Poached Local Sea Fish)

1 onion, chopped
2 tablespoons olive oil
3 cups fish stock
1/2 cup dry white wine
1 bay leaf
Pinch each of thyme, saffron and fennel seed
1/2 pound each of any three white fish—such as sole, cod, and halibut
    —cubed, boned and skinned
Garlic-buttered French toast rounds
Aioli Sauce—optional

1. Sauté onion in olive oil. Add fish stock, white wine, bay leaf and
   seasonings. Bring to a simmer.
2. Add fish to broth and poach gently for 5 minutes. Transfer with
   slotted spoon to warm serving crock lined with garlic-buttered
   French toast rounds, and serve at once.
3. *Aioli Sauce* may be served on the side.

AIOLI SAUCE

3 cloves garlic, crushed
3 egg yolks
1 cup oil
Salt and pepper to taste
Lemon juice to taste

Mix garlic with egg yolks. Whisk oil in *slowly*, as in making mayonnaise.
Season with salt, pepper, and lemon juice after sauce thickens.

DAUBE CAMARGUISE
(Beef Stew with Olives)

2 pounds lean boneless beef chuck, cubed
2 tablespoons olive oil
1 calf's foot, split
1 onion, chopped
3 cloves garlic, crushed
2 tomatoes, peeled, seeded and chopped
1 bay leaf
Pinch each of thyme, salt and freshly ground pepper
1 bottle red wine
4 strips bacon, diced
1 tablespoon butter
1 dozen each: small boiling onions, green olives, black olives

1. Preheat oven to 300 degrees.
2. Dry beef cubes on towels, then brown in flameproof crock
   casserole in olive oil. Add calf's foot, onion, garlic, tomatoes, bay leaf,
   seasonings and wine. Cover and place in preheated oven for 2 hours.
3. Meanwhile, sauté bacon in butter. Add onions and olives; sauté
   gently for 10 minutes.
4. After casserole has cooked for 2 hours, add sautéed bacon, onions
   and olives. Cook 30 minutes longer.
5. Remove calf's foot, adjust seasonings and serve.

COURGETTES AU VERT
(Spinach and Zucchini Sauté)

Pinch of salt
6 zucchini, scrubbed and grated
2 bunches spinach, stemmed and washed
1 onion, chopped
3 tablespoons olive oil
3 tablespoons butter

1. Mix salt with zucchini and let drain.
2. Place spinach in boiling salted water for 3 minutes. Drain and chop.
3. Saute´ onion in olive oil and butter until translucent .
4. Squeeze out liquid from zucchini and spinach and add vegetables to onions. Cook until tender, yet still crisp—about 3 minutes.
5. Salt and pepper to taste, and serve.

PROFITEROLES AU CHOCOLAT
(Cream-filled Puffs with Chocolate Sauce)

1 recipe *Pastry Dough*
1 recipe *Filling*
1 recipe *Topping*

PASTRY DOUGH

1/2 cup soft butter
1 cup water
1 tablespoon sugar
Pinch grated nutmeg
Pinch salt
1 generous cup flour
4 eggs, beaten

1. Preheat oven to 400 degrees.
2. Place butter, water, sugar, nutmeg and salt in a pot. Start over low heat and bring to a boil. Add flour, and beat into a ball. Remove from heat.

3. Add beaten eggs and mix thoroughly.
4. Place *Pastry Dough* in pastry tube and pipe out small balls onto greased baking sheet. Bake in preheated oven for about 20 minutes. Cool on rack while proceeding with *Filling* and *Topping*.

FILLING

1/2 cup sugar
1 tablespoon cornstarch
2/3 cup milk
1 egg yolk
1 vanilla bean
1-1/4 tablespoons Kirsch
1/3 cup heavy cream, beaten stiff

1. Blend sugar, cornstarch and milk and bring to a boil, stirring constantly. Cook until thickened.
2. Remove from heat and mix in egg yolk, vanilla bean and Kirsch. Cool.
3. Remove bean and fold in whipped cream.
4. Fill pastry tube with *Filling* and pipe into slit made in side of each pastry shell.

TOPPING (Chocolate Sauce)

2 8-ounce bars Lanvin dark chocolate
1 tablespoon water
3 tablespoons Kirsch
2 tablespoons sweet butter, melted

1. Melt chocolate in double boiler. Add water, Kirsch and melted butter.
2. Mix thoroughly, cool and serve over filled pastry shells.

Old Bath House
RESTAURANT

Dinner for Four

Escargots de Bourgogne

Cream of Mushroom with Clam Soup

Fresh Spinach and Bacon Salad
with Julio's Dressing

Veal Piccata Ramírez

Tomatoes Florentine

Mocha Marble Cheesecake

Cappuccino

Wines:

With Appetizer, Soup & Salad: Louis Jadot Pouilly-Fuissé
With Entreés: Mont-Redon Châteauneuf-du-Pape

David R. Bindel, Owner
Julio J. Ramírez, Executive Chef

At the turn of the century this wonderful old building on Lover's Point in Pacific Grove, overlooking Monterey Bay, was a popular bath house containing an indoor swimming pool, locker rooms and other assorted recreational activities. Later it became a short-order eatery, then a local seafood cafe. Now, thanks to David Bindel, it is one of the most attractive Continental restaurants in the area.

In 1976 the old dining area was enlarged and decorated in turn-of-the-century Victorian style. In keeping with the building's fascinating origin, it was renamed the Old Bath House, and has since become famous for French and Italian cuisine.

No small credit in this fame is due chef Julio J. Ramirez, a native of Nicaragua, who received his early culinary training with master chef Busquet in Valencia, Spain. Julio came to the Monterey Peninsula and to the Old Bath House shortly after it opened, and his specialties have been pleasing a very demanding public ever since.

"I feel free when I cook," Julio says with enthusiasm, "and I am always looking for a better way to prepare a dish. A meal should be a celebration for *all* the senses."

Dining at the Old Bath House Restaurant is just such a celebration.

620 Ocean View—Lover's Point
Pacific Grove

ESCARGOTS DE BOURGOGNE

20 imported French escargots, canned
20 escargot shells
Dry vermouth to cover
Bourguignonne Butter
French bread

1. Drain escargots, rinse in cold water. Submerge in bowl of dry vermouth to keep moist until ready to use.
2. Assemble escargot shells and partially stuff each with *Bourguignonne Butter.* Then stuff each shell with an escargot, making sure snail goes in head first, foot last. Top each with more *Bourguignonne Butter* and refrigerate until ready to cook.
3. Place shells upside down with opening upright on escargot plate and bake at 400 degrees for 8 minutes.
4. Serve hot with French bread.

Tip: If you do not have an escargot plate, use pie pans filled with rock salt or Marguerita salt to hold shells upright.

BOURGUIGNONNE BUTTER

1/2 pound sweet butter
2 tablespoons minced garlic
1 tablespoon chopped shallots
2 teaspoons chopped parsley
3 tablespoons ground almonds
1 teaspoon salt
3/4 teaspoon ground white pepper
2 tablespoons dry vermouth

Mix all ingredients together in a food processor or bowl.

CREAM OF MUSHROOM WITH CLAM SOUP

1/4 pound butter
1/4 cup minced onions
1 stalk celery, chopped fine
1-1/2 pounds mushrooms, sliced
1 pound clams, chopped
Pinch salt
1/2 teaspoon black pepper
1 quart clam juice
1 cup heavy cream
2 tablespoons sweet butter

1. Melt butter in heavy-bottomed pot. Add onions, celery, mushrooms, clams and salt, and sauté until tender.
2. Add clam juice and cook until liquid is reduced to 3 cups.
3. Add cream and heat slowly until mixture begins to simmer. Remove from heat.
4. Stir in sweet butter and serve.

FRESH SPINACH AND BACON SALAD

1/2 pound bacon, chopped
1 bunch fresh spinach
Julio's Dressing
Garnish: 2 tomatoes, cut into wedges
               2 eggs, hard-boiled and cut into wedges

1. Cook bacon until crisp. Drain on paper towels.
2. Soak spinach in cold water to clean. Drain well.
3. Place spinach and about 3/4 of bacon into bowl. Mix with *Dressing*.
4. Place salad onto individual plates and garnish with 3 wedges of tomato and 3 egg slices. Sprinkle with remaining bacon.

JULIO'S DRESSING

1 clove garlic, mashed
1 egg
1 tablespoon catsup
1/2 teaspoon salt
1/4 teaspoon paprika
Pinch white pepper
1 cup oil
1/4 cup wine vinegar
1 tablespoon water

Blend all ingredients in food processor or blender, and chill well. Blend again or shake well just before serving.

VEAL PICCATA RAMIREZ

1 veal rib-eye, well-trimmed
Salt and pepper
Flour to dredge
3 ounces butter
2 teaspoons chopped shallots
1/4 teaspoon minced garlic
4 teaspoons capers and their juice
2 ounces white wine
1 cup veal or chicken stock
6 canned artichoke hearts, halved to make 12 sections
1 teaspoon lemon juice

1. Slice rib-eye into 12 scallops. Pound each gently. Season with salt and pepper and coat with flour, shaking off any excess.
2. Using 2 sauté pans, melt 1-1/2 ounces butter in each pan—or, if using only 1 pan, go through the process twice. Sauté scallops over fairly high heat to prevent dryness, being careful not to burn butter. Brown 1 side and turn.
3. Add to each pan 1 teaspoon shallots, 1/8 teaspoon minced garlic, 2 teaspoons capers and their juice, 1 ounce white wine, 1/2 cup veal or chicken stock, and 6 artichoke heart halves.
4. Reduce liquid to 1/4 cup and remove from heat. Sprinkle 1/2 teaspoon fresh lemon juice over scallops in each pan and serve.

Use only water-packed artichokes for this dish.

TOMATOES FLORENTINE

4 tomatoes
1 cup half-and-half
1 teaspoon salt
Pinch pepper
Pinch nutmeg
4 egg yolks, beaten
1/2 cup chopped fresh spinach
2 tablespoons grated Parmesan cheese
2 drops Tabasco
2 drops lemon juice

1. Core tomatoes to remove seeds. Set aside.
2. Bring half-and-half, salt, pepper and nutmeg to a simmer. Add egg yolks and spinach. Simmer 10 minutes. Remove from heat and let cool.
3. Add 1 tablespoon Parmesan, Tabasco and lemon juice. Mixture should have a paste-like consistency.
4. Stuff tomatoes with spinach mixture and sprinkle tops with remaining Parmesan cheese.
5. Bake in 350 degree oven for 20 minutes and serve.

MOCHA MARBLE CHEESECAKE

1/3 pound cream cheese
1/3 cup sugar
1-1/2 cups sour cream
1/2 teaspoon vanilla extract
1/2 cup espresso coffee
2 ounces Kahlúa
4 eggs, well-beaten
Garnish: semi-sweet chocolate shavings

1. Blend cream cheese and sugar together in electric mixer.
2. Add sour cream, vanilla, espresso, Kahlúa and eggs. Mix just until blended, being careful not to overmix.
3. Pour cheese mixture into prepared *Cookie Crust.*
4. Bake at 350 degrees for 40 minutes.
5. Chill before serving. Garnish with chocolate shavings.

COOKIE CRUST

1/2 pound Oreo cookies, fillings removed
1 ounce butter, melted

1. Finely crush cookies and mix with melted butter.
2. Press mixture firmly into standard-size pie pan.

CAPPUCCINO

12 ounces espresso coffee, hot
12 ounces half-and-half
2 ounces Amaretto liqueur
2 ounces brandy
4 teaspoons cocoa mix
4 teaspoons sugar
1 ounce vanilla extract
2 ounces whipped cream topping
1 teaspoon chocolate shavings

1. Mix coffee, half-and-half, liqueurs, cocoa mix, sugar and vanilla.
2. Heat and pour into cups. Top with whipped cream and chocolate shavings.

Dinner for Four

Champignons Frits

Griesnockerl Suppe

Salad "Mimosa"
with
Gernot's Salad Dressing

Veal Cordon Bleu

Soufflé Glacé Old Europe

Wines:

With Appetizer: Gewurztraminer, 1977
With Entrée: Dole du Valais, 1975
With Dessert: Johannisberger Riesling Spätlese, 1976

Gernot Leitzinger, Owner & Chef

Dining with Gernot and Rosemarie Leitzinger at the Old Europe Restaurant is like being in a small, charming European inn. The Leitzingers created their restaurant on Pacific Grove's Lighthouse Avenue in 1975 and have delivered excellent cuisine and warm hospitality ever since.

Chef Gernot does all the marketing, then cooks and bakes all of the wonderful food. Hostess Rosemarie and her waitresses, complementing the European picture with their lovely dirndl dresses and happy dispositions, keep the service efficient and unobtrusive. The restaurant's decor has a country-style elegance about it, achieved with crisp and colorful table linens, softly lit chandeliers and a glowing fireplace. Subdued European melodies are heard in the background.

Gernot Leitzinger served his chef's apprenticeship in his native Austria and gained further experience working in hotels and restaurants in Switzerland, Holland and France. "I've been working with food all my life . . . I cook everything from scratch—in the way I was taught by senior European chefs. Our wine selection is appropriate to complement our menu. To make the dining-out experience completely successful, the atmosphere and service must be gracious and pleasant. This I leave to my wife."

"It's like our home and we want our customers to feel welcome and comfortable here, too," adds Rosemarie.

This is the Leitzinger philosophy . . . and it works.

663 Lighthouse Avenue
Pacific Grove

CHAMPIGNONS FRITS

1/2 pound fresh mushrooms
1/2 cup flour
1 egg, beaten
1 cup breadcrumbs
2 cups oil
Tartar Sauce
Garnish: lemon wedges

1. Wash and quarter mushrooms. Bread them by dipping first in flour,
   then in egg, then in breadcrumbs.
2. Fry mushrooms in hot oil until golden brown.
3. Scoop out mushrooms with a strainer, letting excess oil drip off.
4. Serve with *Tartar Sauce* and lemon wedges.

TARTAR SAUCE

1/2 cup mayonnaise
1 dill pickle, chopped
Chopped chives, onion, or green onions—just enough to taste
Pickle juice, as needed

Mix the first 3 ingredients thoroughly. If mixture seems too thick,
add a little pickle juice or vinegar.

***This is a tantalizing appetizer, but it can also be served as a meatless
lunch along with a crisp green salad and French bread.***

GRIESNOCKERL SUPPE

Griesnockerl
1 quart clear chicken or beef bouillon
Sprinkle of chives

1. Prepare *Griesnockerl*. Set aside.
2. Heat chicken or beef bouillon.
3. Combine with *Griesnockerl* and serve hot, sprinkled with chives.

GRIESNOCKERL (Austrian Dumplings for Soup)

1 egg
2-1/2 ounces butter
Dash salt
Dash ground nutmeg
1 tablespoon chopped parsley
3-1/2 ounces Cream of Wheat—regular, not instant

1. Beat egg, butter, salt, nutmeg and parsley together 2 minutes.
2. Add Cream of Wheat and whip 1 minute more. Cover and allow to set 1 hour.
3. With a teaspoon, form oval-shaped dumplings no bigger than bowl of spoon. Place in slightly salted boiling water. Cover and bring back to boil; boil 3 minutes. Lower heat and simmer 12 minutes. Dumplings will rise to 3 times their original size.
4. Remove and serve in hot bouillon, as directed above.

Tip: To test doneness, cut a dumpling in half; if the middle is hard, let them simmer longer.

SALAD "MIMOSA"

Butter lettuce, enough for 4 plates
Gernot's Salad Dressing
Garnish: 1 tomato, peeled and diced
                2 hard-boiled eggs, quartered

1. Wash and spin-dry lettuce until no drops of water are left on leaves.
2. Toss with *Dressing.*
3. Place on individual salad plates and garnish with tomato and egg.

GERNOT'S SALAD DRESSING

1 tablespoon dill weed
1 tablespoon Italian seasoning
1/4 cup water
1/2 teaspoon salt
1/2 teaspoon sugar
2 cloves garlic, chopped
1/2 teaspoon black pepper
1 tablespoon mustard
1/4 cup apple cider vinegar
2 cups vegetable oil

1. Mix dill weed and Italian seasoning in small saucepan with water and
   bring to a boil. Set aside.
2. In container with a tight-fitting lid, mix salt, sugar, garlic, pepper,
   mustard, and vinegar. Add oil and water/seasoning mixture.
   Shake well.

VEAL CORDON BLEU

8 veal cutlets
8 ham slices
4 Swiss cheese slices
1/2 cup flour
2 eggs, beaten
2 cups breadcrumbs
1/2 cup vegetable oil
2 tablespoons butter, melted
Garnish: 4 lemon slices
            1 teaspoon chopped fresh parsley

1. Pound cutlets to 1/4-inch thickness. Cover each with 2 slices of ham and 1 slice of cheese of a size to leave about 1/4-inch around the edges of the cutlets uncovered.
2. Top with remaining 4 cutlets. Press around edges to seal in ham and cheese.
3. Dip each cutlet sandwich in flour to coat, then in egg, and finally in breadcrumbs.
4. Preheat oven to 400 degrees.
5. Pan fry cutlet packets in hot oil until golden brown on both sides. Remove from pan and pat dry. Drizzle with melted butter. Place in preheated oven for 2 minutes to melt cheese.
6. Garnish with lemon slices and parsley.

SOUFFLE GLACE, OLD EUROPE

1 cup whipping cream
1/2 cup sugar
3 egg yolks and 1 whole egg
Grated rind from 1 orange
1/2 cup Grand Marnier
1 ounce macaroon crumbs
1 teaspoon vanilla extract
Garnish: cocoa powder
              powdered sugar

1. Whip cream with half the sugar until stiff.
2. In separate bowl, whip eggs and remaining sugar until fluffy.
3. Add whipped cream and all other ingredients. Set aside.
4. Prepare soufflé dishes: wrap waxed paper collar around rim of dish, about 2 inches high.
5. Divide filling among dishes, and set to freeze at least 4 hours.
6. When ready to serve, remove collar. Sprinkle with cocoa powder and powdered sugar.

Tip: This soufflé can also be prepared in one large soufflé dish.

Dinner for Four

Cold Boiled Shrimp
with
Tangy Cocktail Sauce

Scallops Fondue

Onion Soup Lamar

Salad on the Alley
with
Herbed Dressing "La Flora"

Filet Monterey

Fresh Strawberries Melba

Wines:

With Appetizer: Monterey Vineyards Johannisberg Riesling
With Entrée: Mirassou Petite Sirah

Glenn Hammer, Director of Food & Beverage
Helen Forbes, Manager
Charles W. (Chuck) Peters, Executive Chef

A gourmet restaurant located within a tourist-oriented convention center, is a rarity, but Peter B's in the Doubletree Inn at Fisherman's Wharf in Monterey is just that. Peter B's is the creation of two young food wizards, whose training and accomplishments are most impressive.

The decor, the accoutrements and the ambiance are all due to the skill and planning of Wolfgang Dix. Mr. Dix began his chef's training in Germany. Later, as chief steward aboard a round-the-world luxury liner, he learned the fine points of food and beverage management. He further polished his talents in some of the demanding restaurants of London.

Seeking innovativeness and openness, Mr. Dix selected an American chef, Charles W. (Chuck) Peters, a native of California who graduated cum laude from the Culinary Institute of America and is an Escoffier Award winner. He is also an accredited lecturer and teacher, demonstrating and sharing his knowledge with others. His credits read like a list of the finest restaurants in the nation: Huntington House, Long Island, New York; Harrah's, Lake Tahoe; Hyatt Regency, San Francisco; Cuyamaca Club, San Diego; Maxim Hotel, Las Vegas; and many more.

"We set out to create deliciously different dining in an atmosphere of casual elegance." They have succeeded.

Doubletree Inn, Fisherman's Wharf
Monterey

COLD BOILED SHRIMP

Use this cocktail sauce not only for shrimp but for crabmeat cocktails, poached scallops and deep-fried vegetables as well.

TANGY COCKTAIL SAUCE

2 cups tomato-type chili sauce
1 cup tomato catsup
1/4 cup prepared horseradish
1 teaspoon black pepper
3 tablespoons lemon juice
Dash Worcestershire

Blend all ingredients together and chill.

Tip: This recipe yields nearly 1 quart.

SCALLOPS FONDUE

20 jumbo scallops
Lemon juice to season
1 cup flour
1 quart *Beer Batter*
1-1/2 pints *Cheese Fondue*
Oil for deep frying

1. Season scallops with lemon juice, and lightly dust in flour.
2. Heat oil in a deep fryer to 360 degrees.
3. Dip scallops individually in *Beer Batter* and deep fry to a golden brown, about 4 minutes per scallop.
4. Serve on doilied platter accompanied with small individual ramekin of *Cheese Fondue* for each guest.

(continued on next page)

BEER BATTER

3 cups flour
2 eggs, whole
1/2 cup milk
10 ounces beer
1 teaspoon baking powder
1/2 teaspoon salt
1/4 teaspoon pepper

Blend all ingredients and whisk well.

Tip: Double acting baking powder will allow batter to be stored in the refrigerator for use another time.***

CHEESE FONDUE

1/4 cup butter
1 cup flour
2 cups half-and-half
1/2 cup mozzarella cheese
1 cup Cheddar cheese
1/8 cup Kirsch
1/8 cup white wine
Pinch each salt, pepper and nutmeg

1. Blend butter and flour over low heat to make a roux for thickening.
2. Heat half-and-half; thicken with roux.
3. Add cheeses, Kirsch, wine, salt, pepper and nutmeg.
4. Serve hot in individual ramekins.

The Doubletree Inn's succulent sea scallops are as tender and grand as the acclaimed Bay scallops.

ONION SOUP LAMAR

This can be prepared in advance.

1/4 cup butter
1 pound yellow onions, peeled and sliced
2 tablespoons sweet paprika
1/2 teaspoon white pepper
1/4 cup flour, sifted
3 quarts hot water
1 ounce dry beef bouillon
Salt to taste—optional
6 ounces dark beer
4 large croutons
4 slices mozzarella cheese
4 teaspoons grated Parmesan cheese
Garnish: 4 green onions, chopped

1. Melt butter in heavy kettle. Sauté sliced onions 10 minutes.
2. Add paprika and pepper, stirring mixture 30 seconds.
3. Add flour and bind; do not brown. Cook 3 minutes.
4. Add hot water and beef bouillon, or equivalent amount of beef consommé. Simmer 10 minutes. Consistency should be velvety and smooth. Salt may be added at this point, to taste.
5. Remove from heat. Add beer and marinate in refrigerator overnight. Reheat on top of range before serving.
6. Serve in crockery-type earthenware soup cups. Top each cup with toasted crouton the same size as cup's opening. Place slice of mozzarella cheese and one teaspoon grated Parmesan on top of crouton. Set cups beneath broiler to melt cheeses. Remove and garnish with crisp chopped green onions.

The beer makes the difference! It's our signature Onion Soup for the Doubletree Inns, originally concocted by an old hand in the kitchen whose name—obviously—was Lamar.

SALAD ON THE ALLEY

Artichoke hearts, quartered
Fresh mushrooms, quartered
Herbed Dressing "La Flora"
Leaf, Bibb, iceberg and romaine lettuce
Garnish: 4 slices tomato
            finely chopped parsley

1. Marinate artichoke hearts and mushrooms in *Herbed Dressing "La Flora."*
2. Wash assorted greens thoroughly and dry well. (Reserve curly leaves for plates.) Tear remaining greens into bite-size pieces, cover, and crisp in refrigerator.
3. Line 4 salad plates with curly leaf lettuce.
4. Toss remainder of greens with marinated vegetables in *Herbed Dressing.* Place atop lettuce bed on salad plates.
5. Garnish with tomato and parsley.

HERBED DRESSING "LA FLORA"

4 egg yolks
1 teaspoon freshly cracked black pepper
1 teaspoon garlic salt
1 pint salad oil
Fresh parsley, finely chopped
1/2 cup vinegar
Juice of 1/2 lemon

1. Beat egg yolks in mixing bowl. Add pepper and garlic salt.
2. Slowly blend in salad oil to emulsify.
3. Add chopped parsley.
4. Slowly add vinegar and lemon juice.
5. Whisk together until well blended.

FILET MONTEREY

Be sure you deal with a reputable fish market and select only the freshest fish.

12 raw shrimp
4 ounces crabmeat
12 fresh scallops
Lemon juice
1/2 cup butter
Garlic
Shallots
4 4-ounce filet mignons
8 mushrooms, quartered
8 artichoke hearts, quartered
1 cup white wine
2 cups *Bordelaise Sauce*
Salt and white pepper

1. Peel and devein shrimp. Wash crab and scallops in lemon juice.
2. Melt 1/2 cup butter in sauté pan. Add garlic and shallots and simmer until limp.
3. Pan fry or broil filets and set aside.
4. Quickly sauté seafood together, turning shrimp and scallops. Add mushrooms, artichoke hearts and lemon juice. Add white wine.
5. Finish with addition of *Bordelaise Sauce.* Season with salt and pepper.

To serve—

Place filets on serving dish or platter and arrange seafood and accompanying vegetables around steaks. Glaze all with *Bordelaise Sauce.*

BORDELAISE SAUCE

4 shallots, finely chopped
1 cup red wine
2 cups *Brown Sauce*
1/4 cup beef marrow, poached
1/2 teaspoon chopped tarragon

1. Add shallots to wine and cook until reduced by three-quarters.
2. Add *Brown Sauce* and simmer gently 10 minutes.
3. Just before serving, add marrow and tarragon.

BROWN SAUCE—MADE EASY

1 onion, chopped
1 celery stalk, chopped
1 carrot, chopped
1 clove garlic, chopped
2 tablespoons butter
1/3 cup flour
4 cans bouillon, or beef consommé—32-ounces
4 ounces canned tomato purée or sauce
Bay leaf
Pinch cracked black pepper
Salt

1. Chop all vegetables and place in a small saucepan with melted butter. Sauté 15 minutes or until vegetables are clear.
2. Add flour to bind.
3. Add consommé and tomato purée. Add bay leaf and pepper. *Do not add salt at this time.*
4. Simmer 30 minutes.
5. Strain sauce by using small strainer with fine mesh. Place sauce back on heat and simmer, adding more thickening agent, such as roux.
6. Add salt to taste.

FRESH STRAWBERRIES MELBA

1 pint rich vanilla ice cream
6 fresh strawberries
Curaçao
Brandy
1/2 cup raspberry puree
1/2 cup whipping cream, whipped
4 Gaufrette (Friande Bretagne)

1. Place 2 dollops ice cream in each of 4 wine goblets or other appropriate dessert dishes.
2. Slice strawberries in half and sprinkle over ice cream.
3. Splash a hint of Curaçao and brandy over all.
4. Top with raspberry purée and whipped cream.
5. Garnish with rolled European cookies (Gaufrette).

Both raspberry pureé—or 'melba'—and Pepperidge Farm's Gaufrette-type cookies are sold in most grocery stores.

Raffaello
RESTAURANT

Dinner for Four

Prosciutto and Melon

Fettuccine alla Romana

Petti di Pollo alla Fiorentina

*Romaine Salad
with
Oil and Lemon Dressing*

Zabaglione

Wines:

*With Prosciutto & Fettuccine: Italian Soave or
California Chardonnay
With Entrée: Italian Bardolino or
California Cabernet Sauvignon*

*Remo d'Agliano, Owner/Executive Chef
Amelia d'Agliano, Chef*

The moment you step into Raffaello's you are struck by the atmosphere of competent elegance. Each of the thirteen tables in this intimate restaurant sparkles with silver, crystal, snow-white linens and bowls of fresh-cut flowers. Reservations are necessary, jackets are required for gentlemen, and owner Remo d'Agliano has the kind of personality that makes each diner at Raffaello's feel very special. The atmosphere, although formal, is warm and friendly—a rare combination of class and good fellowship.

Remo came to the Peninsula from Italy in 1964. He and his mother Amelia opened their restaurant in 1965, naming it in honor of Raffaello d'Agliano, Remo's father. (Remo represents the third generation in his family who have been chefs and restaurateurs.) His culinary training and experience took him from Paris to Switzerland, London, Scotland and finally—and fortunately—to Carmel. Honors and awards include membership in the prestigious Accademia Italiana Della Cucina, and the title of Maître Rotisseur, awarded by France's oldest organization of cuisine, the Chaine des Rotisseurs.

Remo's personal touch and talents as owner and chef and those of Amelia, who assists him in the kitchen, have won them the Holiday Magazine Award every year since 1972 and Mobil Guide's Four-Star Award every year since 1973.

Remo says, "We offer from our menu a simple but elegant meal for you to make at home. We hope you will serve our menu for yourselves or friends, and that you will enjoy from beginning to end."

Mission Street, South of Ocean Avenue
Carmel

PROSCIUTTO AND MELON

8 thin slices Italian prosciutto
1 ripe melon, any kind except watermelon
Freshly ground pepper

1. Detach the melon from the rind and cut into wedges.
2. Arrange the prosciutto over the top of the melon. Or, if you
   prefer, roll the prosciutto into paper-thin rolls and serve 2 with
   each slice of melon.
3. Serve with freshly ground pepper.

***If the Italian prosciutto is not available, use Virginia or country
ham, sliced in the same manner.***

***If melon is truly out of season, then pears, figs or even avocado will
substitute very nicely.***

FETTUCCINE ALLA ROMANA

1/2 pound butter, softened
1 egg yolk
1/4 cup heavy cream
1/2 cup freshly grated Parmesan cheese
1 tablespoon salt
1 pound fresh *Fettuccine*
Salt and pepper

1. Beat the butter until light and fluffy. Slowly add the egg yolk
   and cream, beating constantly. Add grated cheese, a few tablespoons
   at a time, beating after each addition.
2. In a large pan, bring approximately 8 quarts of water to a boil; add
   salt and very gently drop in the *Fettuccine.* Stir with a wooden
   spoon for a few moments to separate the noodles, and cook for
   about 7 minutes, or until tender. The pasta should be al dente.
3. Drain the *Fettuccine* into a colander and place in a large heated
   serving bowl. Add the creamed butter and cheese immediately; toss
   very gently and season generously with salt and pepper.

Raffaello

FETTUCCINE NOODLES

1 pound sifted all-purpose flour
3 eggs
1 teaspoon salt
Water

1. Pour flour onto a pastry board, making a well in the center. Place eggs and salt in the well and mix quickly with your fingers until you have a rough ball. Add a little water until you have a firm ball.
2. Knead with your fingers for 10 to 15 minutes, adding extra flour if dough seems sticky. The dough should be smooth and elastic. Cover the dough with a bowl and let it rest for 20 minutes.
3. Divide the dough into 3 or 4 pieces and roll out as thinly as possible on a lightly floured board. Sprinkle the dough with flour and cut into strips about 1/2-inch wide. Spread on a cloth and let dry for about 1 hour before cooking.

The secret of making good fettuccine is using fresh homemade noodles, which in most large cities can be obtained at Italian delicatessans or pasta factories if you don't have time to make your own. Dried fettuccine is not recommended.

PETTI DI POLLO ALLA FIORENTINA

4 chicken breasts, skinned and boned
Salt
Freshly ground black pepper
Flour
3 tablespoons butter
2 tablespoons oil
8 thin 2" by 4" slices prosciutto
8 thin 2" by 4" slices Fontina or Bel Paese cheese
4 teaspoons freshly grated imported Parmesan cheese
2 tablespoons chicken stock

1. Preheat oven to 350 degrees.
2. With a very sharp knife, carefully slice each chicken breast in half
   horizontally to make 8 thin slices. Lay them an inch or so apart on
   a long strip of waxed paper and cover them with another strip of
   waxed paper. Pound the chicken slices lightly with the flat side
   of a cleaver or the bottom of a heavy bottle.
3. Strip off the paper. Season the slices with salt and a few grindings
   of pepper, then dip in flour and shake off the excess.
4. In a heavy pan, melt the butter with the oil over moderate heat.
   Brown the chicken to a light golden brown. Do not overcook.
5. Transfer chicken breasts to a buttered shallow baking dish large
   enough to hold them comfortably. Place a slice of prosciutto and
   then a slice of cheese on each. Sprinkle with grated Parmesan cheese
   and dribble chicken stock over tops. Bake uncovered in the middle
   of the oven for about 10 minutes, or until cheese is melted and
   lightly browned.
6. Serve at once.

***It is nice to serve this dish with rice and steamed spinach.
Season the spinach with butter, salt, pepper and a little freshly
ground nutmeg.***

ROMAINE SALAD

1 head romaine lettuce
1 large tomato, peeled and cut into wedges

1. Discarding dark green outer leaves, wash, dry and then crisp lettuce.
2. Toss lettuce and tomato wedges with *Dressing* and serve.

DRESSING

5 tablespoons olive oil
1 tablespoon lemon juice
Salt and pepper to taste
1 teaspoon dill—optional

Combine all ingredients and shake vigorously until well blended.

ZABAGLIONE

Per serving—

2 egg yolks
3 teaspoons sugar
2 ounces dry Marsala

1. In the top of a double boiler, beat the eggs and sugar with a wire
   whisk until thick. Beat in the wine.
2. Place over boiling water and beat vigorously until hot, very thick
   and foamy.
3. Serve immediately.

***It's nice to serve this dessert in tall, attractive glasses. Thin wafers
or cookies go nicely on the side.***

***We suggest, after your dessert, you have espresso, served with
a little fresh lemon peel; or, if you prefer, just good strong coffee.***

Dinner for Six

Fettuccine con Scampi Langoustine

Zuppa di Zucchini

Hearts of Romaine
with
Roquefort Dressing

Veal Cardinal

French Fried Cauliflower

Cannoli

Flaming Sardine

Wines:

With Appetizer and Soup: David Bruce Chardonnay
With Entrée: Jadot Beaujolais Village

Ted Balestreri and Bert Cutino, Owners/Hosts
Bill Lee, Manager
Ranjeet Lal, Chef

In the heyday of the sardine industry on Cannery Row, the building now housing the Sardine Factory was actually a cafeteria for hungry cannery workers. When Ted Balestreri and Bert Cutino joined as partners in 1968, they bought the historic old building and transformed it into one of the most elegant restaurants on the Peninsula. The lush, nostalgic decor is enhanced by fascinating old photographs and other memorabilia from the days when Cannery Row was the 'Sardine Capital of the World.' The Captains' Room recalls the plush ambiance of the 1880's and The Lounge sports a hundred-and-twenty-year-old bar, all hand-carved.

Gerald Peters is executive chef for all of the restaurants owned by Ted and Bert. Gerry has been awarded the Escoffier Medal of Merit and many other top prizes in culinary exhibitions all over the country. Chef Peters, with the aid of manager Bill Lee and chef Ranjeet Lal, has won many awards for the restaurant as well, including The Holiday Magazine Award, Mobil Four-Star Award and high ratings from Town and Country and Gourmet magazines.

Chef Ranjeet Lal was born in the Fiji Islands and is of Hindu-Indian descent. "Consistency in food preparation is the key to the success of my kitchen operation," chef Lal asserts.

701 Wave Street
Monterey

FETTUCINE CON SCAMPI LANGOUSTINE

1 pound fettucine noodles
Fettucini Sauce
Scampi Langoustine

FETTUCINE SAUCE

1/4 pound sweet butter, softened
1 egg yolk
1/4 cup heavy cream
1/2 cup freshly grated Parmesan cheese
Salt
Pepper

1. Beat butter until fluffy. Continue beating and add the egg yolk and then the cream.
2. Finally, beat in the cheese and season with salt and pepper.

SCAMPI LANGOUSTINE

12 Danish baby lobster tails
Clarified butter
1 clove garlic, minced
2 ounces white wine
1 ounce lemon juice
1 tablespoon finely chopped parsley
2 tablespoons whole butter

1. Remove shells from lobsters and de-vein, but leave on the tail section. Dredge lightly in flour and sauté in clarified butter over a high heat.
2. Add garlic, wine, lemon juice and parsley.
3. Remove from heat and mix with whole butter.

Tip: To make clarified butter: melt butter in a double boiler over low heat. Let stand a few minutes allowing solids to settle to bottom and skim clear butter from the top.

To prepare—

1. In a large kettle of salted boiling water, cook fettucine noodles for 7 to 8 minutes or until just tender (al dente). Drain thoroughly.
2. Mix noodles with *Fettucine Sauce* and cook briefly, adding a little heavy cream if necessary, until the sauce becomes a very creamy consistency. Add the *Scampi Sauce* and toss thoroughly.
3. Serve immediately, using 2 scampi per person as garnish for top.

To make clarified butter: melt butter in a double boiler over low heat. Let stand a few minutes allowing solids to settle to bottom and skim clear butter from the top.

ZUPPA DI ZUCCHINI

1-1/2 pounds zucchini
1/4 cup butter
1 medium onion, sliced
7-1/2 cups chicken stock
2 chicken bouillon cubes
2 eggs
3 tablespoons grated Parmesan cheese
2 tablespoons chopped fresh basil
Salt
Black pepper, freshly ground

1. Top and tail the courgettes (zucchini) and cut into 1/4-inch slices.
2. Melt the butter in a large saucepan and fry onion very gently for 5 minutes. Add the courgettes and fry, stirring frequently, for 5 to 10 minutes or until lightly golden.
3. Add the stock, crumble in the bouillon cubes and bring to a boil. Cover and lower the heat to simmer and continue cooking gently for about 20 minutes.
4. Pass the mixture through the coarse mesh of a mouli-legume or sieve, or pureé in an electric blender, then return to the saucepan.
5. Just before serving, bring soup to a boil.

6. Combine the eggs, cheese and basil in the bottom of a large warmed soup tureen. Using a wire whisk, beat together thoroughly. Still whisking, pour the boiling soup slowly into the beaten eggs.
7. Season with salt and pepper and serve immediately. Serve with a separate bowl of Parmesan cheese.

This is a nourishing, yet delicately flavored soup. Although prettily flecked with flakes of egg, it can be reheated the following day, provided it does not boil.

HEARTS OF ROMAINE SALAD

Hearts of romaine for six people, prepared for serving.

ROQUEFORT DRESSING

1/4 pound Roquefort cheese
2 cloves garlic, minced
2 tablespoons finely chopped onions
1/2 cup mayonnaise
2 1/3 cups sour cream
1/2 cup lemon juice
1 teaspoon white pepper
1 teaspoon salt
1-1/3 ounces wine vinegar

1. Grind cheese, garlic and onions together in a blender. Add mayonnaise and mix on low speed for 3 minutes.
2. Add remaining ingredients and mix for 2 more minutes.
3. Serve with hearts of romaine.

Leftover dressing will keep for about 3 weeks in refrigerator.

VEAL CARDINAL

6 6-ounce lobster tails
1-1/4 pounds fine white veal, cut in thin slices
Flour to dredge
2 tablespoons butter
1-1/2 pounds fresh mushrooms, washed and sliced
1/2 cup dry sauterne wine
2 tablespoons finely chopped fresh parsley
Juice of 1 lemon
2 tablespoons finely chopped fresh garlic
Salt and pepper

1. Dip lobster and veal in flour. Heat butter in a skillet and sauté lobster lightly.
2. Add mushrooms and continue cooking until mushrooms are tender.
3. Remove lobster and mushrooms with a slotted spoon and set aside.
4. In the same pan, sauté veal until golden brown on both sides, adding more butter if necessary. Lower heat.
5. Return lobster and mushrooms to skillet. Add wine and touch with a lighted match, cautiously. Let burn down. When flames have subsided, add parsley, lemon juice and garlic. Simmer 2 to 3 minutes.
6. Taste for seasoning and serve.

FRENCH FRIED CAULIFLOWER

1 large head cauliflower
1 cup breadcrumbs
1/2 cup grated Parmesan cheese
2 eggs
3 tablespoons cold water
Salt and pepper
1 1/2 teaspoons fresh sweet basil, if available
Fat, for frying

1. Break the cauliflower into flowerets and cook gently in boiling water for 10 minutes. Drain.
2. Mix bread crumbs with Parmesan cheese; mix the eggs with cold water and beat together. Roll flowerets first in breadcrumbs, then in egg batter, then again in breadcrumbs.
3. Fry in deep hot fat at 375 degrees until browned. Drain on absorbent paper.
4. Sprinkle with salt, pepper and sweet basil and serve very hot.

CANNOLI

7 tablespoons confectioners' sugar, sifted
1 tablespoon butter
1 egg
1/2 cup all-purpose flour, sifted
1-1/2 tablespoons cream sherry
1/2 tablespoon wine vinegar
Fat for deep frying
1/2 pound Ricotta cheese
2 ounces mixed candied fruit, diced
1/2 teaspoon vanilla extract
1/4 teaspoon ground cinnamon
1/2 tablespoon or more heavy cream
Pistachio nuts or maraschino cherries for garnish

1. Mix together 1 tablespoon sugar, butter, egg, flour, sherry and vinegar. If too stiff, add a little water. Let dough stand at room temperature for about 30 minutes.
2. Cut dough into pieces about the size of a walnut. Roll out each piece to an oval shape. Wrap each around an oiled wooden stick about 1 inch in diameter and 6 inches long. Seal the edge with a drop of cold water.
3. Heat the fat to 365 degrees on a frying thermometer.
4. Gently remove the stick and drop each rolled wafer into the fat. Fry until golden brown, lift out carefully, drain, and place on a cake rack to cool.
5. Drain the Ricotta cheese. Be sure it is cold and dry, but not iced. Mix with the remaining 6 tablespoons confectioners' sugar, the candied fruits, vanilla, cinnamon and cream. If the mixture is too thick, add a little more cream. Mix well. Use to fill the cooled wafers.
6. Garnish each end with chopped pistachio nuts or halved maraschino cherries. Sprinkle with confectioners' sugar when ready to serve.

This is a traditional Italian pastry.

FLAMING SARDINE

Per cup—

2 ounces Galliano liqueur
Lime juice
Powdered sugar
Twist of lemon
1 cup hot black coffee

1. Use rather large brandy snifter-type glasses. Rim with lime juice,
    then dip rims into powdered sugar.
2. Pour in 2 ounces Galliano liqueur.
3. Light the Galliano with a flourish and, while it is flaming, twist
    a lemon peel over it.
4. As the sparks fly, drop the peel into the glass and fill with a cup
    of hot, black coffee.

***Make this dramatic drink before your audience, one cup at a
time.***

WHALING STATION INN
RESTAURANT

Dinner for Four

Artichoke Vinaigrette

Gazpacho Soup

Roasted Pacific Red Snapper

Saffron Rice

*Steamed Vegetable in Season
(Sicilian Style)*

*Whaling Station Salad
with
Special Oil Dressing*

St. Joseph's Puff Supreme

Cappuccino

Wines:

*With Appetizer & Soup: Enz Rosé of Zinfandel or
Husch Rosé of Pinot Noir
With Entrée & Salad: Franciscan Chardonnay or
Freemark Abbey Chardonnay*

*John Pisto, Owner/Executive Chef
Bert Simpson, Maître'd
Jess Indracusin, Chef-in-Residence*

In their selection of period wicker furniture and tulip-shaped chandeliers in the bar-lounge, with elegant dark paneling and seafaring motif in the dining area, John and Cheryl Pisto have created an imaginative setting for their restaurant overlooking famed Cannery Row.

John Pisto uses no less imagination to create a truly delectable regional cuisine. He supplies his kitchen with foods grown or caught in the Monterey area. On occasion, he and his son may be found searching the nearby hills for the area's special fresh herbs. His oakwood broiler adds a special ingredient to many fine recipes.

Owner and executive chef Pisto is a native Montereño, with all the warmth and openness of that tradition. He apprenticed and became a gourmet chef under skilled and naturally talented local 'paisano' culinary masters. Only after the Whaling Station Inn Restaurant became recognized as a top gourmet dining place did John's insatiable curiosity take him to France to 'brush-up,' as he says, on continental cookery.

763 Wave Street
Monterey

ARTICHOKE VINAIGRETTE

4 medium artichokes, trimmed
Water to cook
1 clove garlic, crushed
1 bay leaf
Salt and pepper to taste
1/2 lemon
Vinaigrette Dressing

1. Stand trimmed artichokes close together in a pot with water measuring halfway to their tops. Add garlic, bay leaf, salt and pepper. Squeeze in lemon juice, then drop in whole lemon rind. Cover.
2. Cook over medium heat until done. Test with a fork inserted into artichoke heart; it should be tender but not mushy.
3. Drain and squeeze out extra water from artichokes. 'Flowerette' by striking top of each artichoke with the palm of your hand, pushing downward to form an open flower. Cut out the 'beard.' Place on round dishes and dress with *Vinaigrette Dressing.*

VINAIGRETTE DRESSING

3/4 cup olive oil
1/4 cup wine vinegar
1/4 teaspoon dry mustard or Dijon mustard
Drop of catsup—optional
Few drops Tabasco, to taste
1 anchovy filet, mashed
Pepper to taste
Pinch sugar
1 clove garlic, mashed or diced very fine

Mix and chill well before using as directed.

Anchovy replaces salt. But taste before adding it all. You must satisfy your personal taste. Remember that saltiness may be added but never taken away!

GAZPACHO SOUP

3 cups whole tomatoes, canned
1/2 cucumber, finely diced
1/2 small white onion, finely diced
1 stalk celery, finely diced
1/4 lime
1/4 orange
1 tablespoon Worcestershire
Salt and pepper to taste
Pinch cumin
Pinch chili powder
Pinch coriander
1 tablespoon cider vinegar
Garnish: croutons

1. Drain off some of the juice from canned tomatoes. Crush tomatoes into thumbnail pieces.
2. Add cucumber, onion and celery to tomatoes.
3. Emulsify lime and orange pieces with rinds in blender. Add to tomato mixture. Season with Worcestershire, salt and pepper, cumin, chili powder, coriander and vinegar. Blend well and chill.
4. Serve very cold, with croutons.

Soup should have bits of vegetables in evidence. This is like a Bloody Mary, and very tasty.

ROASTED PACIFIC RED SNAPPER

8 cloves garlic
2 Pacific red snappers, 3 pounds each—whole, gutted, scaled, and
   trimmed of fins, with heads on
1/4 cup olive oil
Salt and pepper
1 thyme leaf, crushed
1 to 1-1/2 cups fresh anise, tops only
2 cups light fish broth or water—more if needed
3 to 4 ounces Pernod
2 ounces Cognac
Garnish: flat leaf Italian parsley

1. Preheat oven to 475 degrees.
2. Insert garlic, 2 to a side, into fish backs. Rub fish inside and out with
   olive oil, sprinkling well with salt and pepper. Sprinkle outside with
   thyme. Stuff belly cavities with anise.
3. Use remaining anise to cover a rack placed in bottom of a roasting
   pan—a turkey roaster is fine. Position fish on top of anise. Add fish
   broth or water, Pernod, and Cognac. Cover with aluminum foil.
4. Bake in preheated oven until done, about 25 minutes, adding broth
   or water if necessary. Keep checking behind the head with a fork
   for doneness. As soon as flesh begins to look opaque, remove foil,
   bake 10 minutes longer, or until fish is browned. Remove.
5. Bone and serve with unstrained pan juices ladled over fish.
   Garnish with parsley.

Tip: To bone cooked fish: remove head (reserving cheeks, which are a
      delicacy). Slit body of fish laterally, the entire length of the fish,
      with a sharp knife. Then cut horizontally, cutting only to the
      backbone. With a spatula or fish server, lift up each section from
      the top layer of the fish and serve. Then remove the backbone,
      and cut the bottom layer into serving portions.

***We prepare this dish over an open oakwood broiler for our customers,
but for home preparation, roasting in the oven is fine.***

SAFFRON RICE

1/2 cup finely chopped white onion
2 tablespoons olive oil
1 cup Texas long grain or Italian rice
2 cups fish stock
1 bay leaf
Salt and pepper to taste
Pinch of saffron for color

1. Preheat oven to 350 or 400 degrees.
2. Sauté onions in olive oil until glazed. Add rice and stir until grains are translucent. Add fish stock, bay leaf, salt and pepper, and saffron. Bring to a boil and remove from heat.
3. Place rice, uncovered, in preheated oven and cook until done, approximately 20 minutes. Check often to be sure rice does not dry out. Add more fish stock or water if needed.
4. Fluff, and serve.

Tip: Italian rice will need cooking a little longer. Never use converted rice for this recipe.

STEAMED VEGETABLE IN SEASON, SICILIAN STYLE

4 cups of any fresh vegetable in season: broccoli, green beans, zucchini, or whatever is available
1 clove garlic, crushed
2 tablespoons olive oil
1 tablespoon butter
Salt and pepper to taste

1. Steam vegetable until cooked but crunchy, al dente, about 5 to 8 minutes.
2. Sauté garlic in olive oil and butter. Remove garlic and pour oil and butter over vegetables to coat. Salt and pepper to taste and serve hot.

WHALING STATION INN SALAD

1/2 head Romaine lettuce
1 small head Bibb lettuce
1 head Belgian endive
1 bunch watercress
1/2 cup chopped walnut meats
Special Olive Oil Dressing

1. Wash and dry leaves of all greens. Crisp in refrigerator until ready
   to use.
2. Mix in walnut meats, and toss lightly with *Special Olive Oil Dressing.*

SPECIAL OLIVE OIL DRESSING

3/4 cup Marsala brand olive oil
1/8 cup rice vinegar
1/8 cup cider vinegar
Dash lemon juice
Dash Worcestershire
1/4 teaspoon dry mustard

Blend well and use as directed.

***What makes this dressing so special is the olive oil from
Sciabica & Sons, a Sicilian family business in Modesto, California.
This 'Marsala' brand is a virgin cold press olive oil—the finest available.
And there is no better vinegar than rice vinegar to go with it.***

ST. JOSEPH'S PUFF SUPREME

1 recipe *St. Joseph's Puffs*
1 egg yolk, beaten
2 cups fresh fruit: sliced strawberries, raspberries, kiwi fruit, figs
   or peaches
1 recipe *Crème Pâtissière*
1/4 to 1/2 cup whipping cream, stiffly whipped
Sugar to sweeten
1 teaspoon rum
Pinch salt
Powdered sugar

1. Preheat oven to 450 degrees.
2. Fill large pastry tube with puff dough. On an unoiled, unfloured baking sheet, make a 1-inch circle of dough, continuing round and round until one large puff is completed, using all the dough. Lightly smooth the top and brush with beaten egg yolk.
3. Place in preheated oven and bake for 10 minutes. Lower oven heat to 350 degrees and continue baking spiral for 20 minutes more until slightly brown. Remove and cool.
4. With serrated knife, cut pastry in half, removing top. Form a shell by removing inside dough.

To assemble—

Fill first with layer of *Crème Pâtissière,* then a layer of sliced fruit. Top with sweetened whipped cream flavored with rum and a pinch of salt. Decorate with whipped cream, or powder top heavily with powdered sugar. Serve whole, cutting at table into four servings.

ST. JOSEPH'S PUFFS

1 tablespoon butter
Pinch of salt
1/4 cup flour—use only hard, winter wheat flour
1/4 cup water
1 egg
1/4 tablespoon sugar
1/4 tablespoon grated lemon rind
1/4 teaspoon grated orange rind

1. Place water and butter in saucepan. Bring to a boil. Add flour and

stir until mixture leaves sides of pan and forms a ball in the center. Remove from stove and cool.

2. Add egg and beat thoroughly. Add sugar, orange and lemon rinds. Mix well.
3. Use as directed in large pastry tube, or drop by tablespoon on cookie pan 3 inches apart if you prefer individual cream puffs.

Tip: Health food stores can provide the proper flour if your grocery does not stock it.

CREME PATISSIERE

1/2 cup flour
1/3 cup sugar
Pinch salt
2 teaspoons butter
3 egg yolks
1 cup milk
1/2 teaspoon vanilla extract

1. Combine flour, sugar, salt, butter and egg yolks. Mix well.
2. Heat milk, but do not boil, and combine with mixture. Cook until very thick, stirring constantly, for at least 5 minutes. Add vanilla.
3. Cover and chill until ready to assemble *St. Joseph's Puff Supreme.*

CAPPUCCINO

For each cup—

1 cup espresso—Italian black-roast coffee
Dash bitter chocolate syrup
Dash brandy, Amaretto or 1 ounce Samboca
Light cream, to color to a medium dark brown
Sugar to taste
Freshly whipped cream
Sprinkle of cinnamon

1. Prepare espresso in Italian *caffettiera*, or coffeemaker.
2. Add chocolate syrup, brandy, Amaretto or Samboca, cream and sugar. Top with whipped cream, dust with cinnamon.

This drink should be only slightly sweet. The chocolate taste must come through, yet not overpower the coffee.

Will's Fargo Restaurant

Dinner for Four

Fresh Chilled Relish Tray

Beef-Vegetable Soup

*Mixed Greens Salad
with
Avocado Dressing*

Hot Cheddar Cheese Bread

Sautéed Abalone, Morro Bay

Stuffed Baked Potato

Nita's Walnut Pie

Espresso Blended Coffee

Will's Café Yum-Yum

Wine:

Napa Valley Chappellet Pinot Chardonnay, 1975

*Will and Barbara Fay, Owners
Clifford H. Washington, Head Chef*

Will's Fargo at the Carmel Valley Village is about twelve miles east of Carmel on the scenic Carmel Valley Road, and well worth the drive.

Will and Barbara Fay established their restaurant in 1959 in one of the village's oldest buildings, patterned after Father Serra's mission-style architecture. Over the years, Will, Barbara and chef Clifford Washington have made Will's Fargo into an institution on the Peninsula. Barbara describes the decor as Western-Victorian, Will describes the menu as all-American, and chef Washington refuses to sacrifice quality for quantity, emphasizing freshness of ingredients as his most important demand.

Entering through the massive, carved Victorian doors, the warmth and casualness of Will's Fargo puts one immediately at ease. Barbara or Will personally greets the diner at the meat counter where he may supervise the cutting of his own steak. The meat is weighed right there for pricing, then tagged to insure that it will be cooked to the desired degree of doneness. Chef Clifford's talents extend to the preparation of delicious chops, seafoods, sauces, dressings and desserts.

From the before-dinner drink at the charming antique bar in the lobby to the made-from-scratch desserts, the food, the service, and the surroundings are second to none on the Monterey Peninsula.

Carmel Valley Village, Carmel Valley Road
Carmel

RELISH TRAY

Carrot strips
Green onions
Celery hearts or sticks
Green and black olives
Peperoncini

Prepare relishes and arrange attractively on a chilled celery dish,
atop a bed of crushed ice.

***Always use the freshest items available—well-scrubbed, peeled
and chilled.***

BEEF-VEGETABLE SOUP

1/2 pound lean beef—stew meat will do nicely
1-1/2 quarts beef stock
1/2 cup diced carrots
1/2 cup diced celery
1/4 cup chopped white onions
1/4 cup diced potatoes
1/4 cup baby lima beans
1/4 cup green peas
Salt and pepper to taste
Cumin to taste
1/2 crushed bay leaf
Dash Tabasco
1/4 cup chopped parsley

1. Trim sinew and fat from meat and cut into small pieces about the
   size of a small fingernail. Sauté and drain fat, saving the juices.
2. Combine all ingredients, except parsley, with salt, pepper, cumin,
   bay leaf, and a dash of Tabasco.
3. Simmer until vegetables are done, but not mushy. Add parsley.
   Correct seasoning and serve in pre-heated bouillon cups.

MIXED GREENS SALAD WITH AVOCADO DRESSING

1 head romaine lettuce
1 small head endive or chicory
1/2 head iceberg lettuce
Garnish: cherry tomatoes
Avocado Dressing
Cracked pepper to taste

1. Wash and dry greens thoroughly. Remove large outer leaves and tear into bite-size pieces; toss lightly.
2. Fill pre-chilled bowls, such as soup plates.
3. Garnish with cherry tomatoes, and top with *Avocado Dressing,* then lace with freshly cracked pepper.
4. Serve with *Hot Cheddar Cheese Bread.*

AVOCADO DRESSING

1 large *ripe* avocado, mashed
1/2 pint sour cream
1/2 cup Best Foods mayonnaise
2 tablespoons wine vinegar
1 teaspoon Lea and Perrins
2 tablespoons lemon juice
1 tablespoon chopped chives
1 tablespoon chopped parsley
1 teaspoon Lawry's seasoning salt—optional
Salt and pepper to taste

1. Combine all ingredients. Cover and store in refrigerator for 3 hours.
2. Remove 1/2 hour before serving. Correct seasoning and top the salad greens, using all the dressing.

***If a greener color is desired, increase the amount of minced parsley in the *Avocado Dressing.* ***

HOT CHEDDAR CHEESE BREAD

8 thin slices sourdough bread
1 pound Wispride Cheddar cheese, softened
1/4 pound butter
1/4 cup grated Parmesan cheese
1 tablespoon paprika, preferably Hungarian

Blend together cheeses, butter and paprika. Spread on sourdough bread slices.

You may wish to toast one side of the bread first, before spreading cheese mixture on untoasted side.

SAUTEED ABALONE, MORRO BAY

4 large white abalone steaks
1 cup or more cracker meal
4 tablespoons butter, divided into equal portions per steak

1. Using coarse side of tenderizing hammer, pound each steak on both sides, being careful not to perforate.
2. Dredge in cracker meal.
3. Heat butter in two skillets; just as butter begins to brown, add abalone, cooking 30 seconds on each side.
4. Blot each steak with paper towel before transferring to dinner plate.

It is best to do no more than two steaks at a time, one to a skillet.

STUFFED BAKED POTATOES

4 large russet baking potatoes
1/2 cup light cream, warmed
1 teaspoon Colman's mustard
1 tablespoon minced green onion
2 tablespoons grated Parmesan cheese
1 tablespoon butter
Salt and white pepper, to taste
Sour cream and chopped bacon bits if desired

1. Preheat oven to 400 degrees.
2. Bake potatoes until done, approximately 1 hour.
3. Make a deep slit down top of each potato; grasp with a hot pad and, using a soupspoon, scoop out the 'meat' of the potato, being careful not to break the skin. Reserve skins.
4. Place potato meat into a mixing bowl, add all ingredients and mix well. Correct seasoning.
5. Stuff mixture back into empty skins with soupspoon until original slit is sealed; potato should look like its original shape.
6. Reheat in 400 degree oven for 20 minutes.
7. Serve with sour cream and chopped bacon bits if desired.

Potatoes should not be refrigerated, but may be prepared in the morning and wrapped in foil until ready to reheat. Remove foil, reheat and serve as indicated.

NITA'S WALNUT PIE

10" pie crust, unbaked
4 eggs
1-3/4 cups walnuts
1-1/2 cups dark Karo
3/4 cup sugar
2 tablespoons flour
Dash of salt
2 teaspoons vanilla extract
5 tablespoons butter, melted
Garnish: whipped cream

1. Preheat oven to 325 degrees.
2. Line a 10" pie plate with crust.
3. Beat together the eggs, walnuts, Karo, sugar, flour and a dash of salt. Add vanilla.
4. Add melted butter and mix well.
5. Bake for 45 to 50 minutes in preheated oven, until set.
6. Remove and serve warm or cold with whipped cream.

ESPRESSO COFFEE BLEND

1 pound Yuban coffee
1/2 pound espresso beans, freshly ground

Blend coffees together. Brew according to favored taste and method.

WILL'S CAFE YUM-YUM

Per serving—

Hot strong coffee
1 ounce coffee-flavored brandy
Partially whipped cream, unflavored and unsweetened
Bittersweet chocolate, grated

Preheat Irish Coffee glass. Add coffee and coffee-flavored brandy, and top with partially whipped cream. Sprinkle with grated bittersweet chocolate.

Do not use swizzlestick!

APPETIZERS

BEVERAGES

BREADS and BATTERS

DESSERTS and DESSERT ACCENTS

ENTREES

PASTA and RICE

SALADS

SALAD DRESSINGS

SAUCES, SPICES and STOCKS

SOUPS

VEGETABLES and SIDE DISHES

A Collection of Gourmet Recipes
From the Finest Chefs in the Country!

If you enjoyed **Dining In—Monterey Peninsula,**
additional volumes are now available:

Please send me the quantity checked:

____ Dining In—San Francisco   ____ Dining In—Seattle
____ Dining In—Chicago   ____ Dining In—Minneapolis/St. Paul
____ Dining In—Houston   ____ Dining In—Los Angeles
                                  ____ Dining In—Monterey Peninsula

(and available by August 1979)

____ Dining In—Dallas   ____ Dining In—San Diego
____ Dining In—Portland

(and available by September 1979)

____ Dining In—St. Louis   ____ Dining In—Philadelphia

TO ORDER SEND $7.95 PLUS $1.00 POSTAGE AND HANDLING FOR EACH BOOK

ORDER FORM

B name _____

I address_____

L city_____ state_____ zip_____

L

       PAYMENT   CHARGE   Visa # _____ Exp. date_____
       ENCLOSED   TO:

T   Master Chg. #_____ Exp. date_____

O   Signature_____

S name _____   name_____

H address _____   address_____

I city_____   city_____

P state & zip_____   state & zip_____

Peanut Butter Publishing, Peanut Butter Towers
2733 - 4th Ave. So., Seattle, WA 98134